What People Are Saying about
Discover Your *True Strength*

Some books teach you the principles needed for that moment of "What do I do?" or an encouraging word to keep you moving forward through the toughest of times. Lindsay Roberts, in *Discover Your True Strength*, not only teaches and encourages but also empowers you with Scripture to obtain the overcomer's stance of peace and stability to stand firm and strong.

—Joni Lamb
Daystar Television Network

I am so happy Lindsay wrote this book, *Discover* Your *True Strength*. Too often we overcomplicate things like hearing God's voice and being led by Him, leaving us confused and doubting, instead of moving forward into all that He has for us. In this practical guidebook, Lindsay gives us the tools we need to discover our true strength so we can walk in even deeper relationship with Him.

—Real Talk Kim (Kim Jones)
Pastor, entrepreneur, mentor, motivational speaker,
and best-selling author

If you're ready to level up your life, you need to read this book! Lindsay gives practical yet powerful principles that will help you tap into your God-given strength and potential and take you from settling to soaring!

—April Osteen Simons
Hope coach

I am excited about Lindsay Roberts's new book. When it comes to helping women overcome obstacles, there are few people who are as experienced and compassionate as Lindsay. Her chapter entitled "Strong Women Bounce Back" is essential reading for any woman who finds herself sitting in a setback. She teaches us that while you are feeling the sting of your setback, God is preparing your comeback.

—Tim Storey
Author, speaker, and life coach

In her book, Lindsay Roberts takes you on a miraculous journey of faith to help you discover your God-given strengths through His Word that will, in turn, bless and strengthen others. As you take practical steps to fulfill your calling, by choosing courage and joy, and by relying on God's supernatural inner strength, you will find you are truly stronger than you think to positively impact your world!

—Lisa Osteen Comes
Associate pastor, Lakewood Church

If you are holding this book, buckle up! Get ready to discover your true strength and accomplish your God-given assignments. Lindsay has done a fabulous job of paving the way with practical tips and truth she has gleaned from years of seeking God's Word and putting it into action. I believe you will finish this book even stronger than when you started!

—Melissa Lee
Cohost, *Make Your Day Count* and *Bookmark*

I've known Lindsay for many years and have found her books to be filled with Bible-based, practical teaching, and to me, *Discover Your True Strength* is following that same pattern. In just the chapter titles alone, it felt like I was navigating a path on a journey to discover true strength that comes from the Lord, identifying strength-stealers, and ultimately finding true "strength in the Lord and in the power of HIS might."

—**Kate McVeigh**
Kate McVeigh Ministries
Speaker and host, *The Voice of Faith* radio program
Author, *The Blessing of Favor* and *Get Over It*

In *Discover Your True Strength*, Lindsay Roberts has created a roadmap for personal transformation and empowerment. As someone who has dedicated her life to helping women to break free from limitations and live their dreams, this book is a powerful tool in that journey.

Each chapter, grounded in faith and biblical wisdom, encourages readers to recognize the incredible strength that resides within them through Christ to rise above every challenge. This isn't just a self-help book; it's an invitation to a life of fulfillment, success, and understanding the extraordinary power you possess in Him.

The inclusion of stories of strong women from the Bible, history, and modern-day heroes adds a relatable and inspiring dimension to the book. It's a testament to the fact that strength and courage are timeless qualities God has placed in you. As you embark on the journey outlined in *Discover Your True Strength*, may you be inspired to embrace new strength, rooted in the Word of God. I believe this book will empower you from the inside out to live a life of impact and success.

—**Terri Savelle Foy**
Author, *The Alone Advantage*

Lindsay's words are inspiring and full of wisdom, and we highly recommend this book to anyone seeking to deepen their relationship with God and discover their true strength in Him. The possibilities God has for each of us are limitless.

Francie and I have enjoyed many prayer calls with Richard and Lindsay, and *Discover Your True Strength* is a reflection of Lindsay's heart to help people see that God is love, that He has given each of us a unique strength and calling, and that through Him, we can truly tap into our full potential. This book has been a blessing to us, and we believe it will be a blessing to many others as well.

—**Duane "Dog the Bounty Hunter" and Francie Chapman**
Public figures and speakers

DISCOVER *YOUR* TRUE STRENGTH

*Choosing to Thrive
in the Midst of
Life's Challenges*

LINDSAY ROBERTS

WHITAKER
HOUSE

Note: This book is not intended to provide medical or psychological advice or to take the place of medical advice and treatment from your personal physician. Those who are having suicidal thoughts or who have been emotionally, physically, or sexually abused should seek help from a mental health professional or qualified counselor. Neither the publisher nor the author nor the author's ministry or business takes any responsibility for any possible consequences from any action taken by any person reading or following the information in this book. If readers are taking prescription medications, they should consult with their physicians and not take themselves off prescribed medicines without the proper supervision of a physician. Always consult your physician or other qualified health care professional before undertaking any change in your physical regimen, whether fasting, diet, medications, or exercise.

DISCOVER *YOUR* TRUE STRENGTH:
Choosing to Thrive in the Midst of Life's Challenges

Lindsay Roberts
http://makeyourdaycount.com
https://richardroberts.org/mydc/

ISBN: 979-8-88769-221-0
eBook ISBN: 979-8-88769-222-7
Printed in the United States of America
© 2024 by Lindsay Roberts

Whitaker House • 1030 Hunt Valley Circle • New Kensington, PA 15068
www.whitakerhouse.com

LC record available at https://lccn.loc.gov/2024000373
LC ebook record available at https://lccn.loc.gov/2024000374

1 2 3 4 5 6 7 8 9 10 11 ⨆⨅ 30 29 28 27 26 25 24

To Jordan, Olivia, and Chloe, my greatest sources of inspiration and strength. You three are my definition of resilience, courage, creativity, intelligence, and unconditional love. It's your unwavering spirit that drives the message of this book. I love you all dearly.

Richard, your steadfast support has been my pillar of strength throughout our marriage and certainly throughout the journey of writing this book. You are the rock of our family, and I love you. Thank you for always being my biggest encourager.

Be strong in the Lord and in the power of His might.
—Ephesians 6:10

I can do all things through Christ who strengthens me.
—Philippians 4:13

The joy of the LORD is your strength.
—Nehemiah 8:10

CONTENTS

Acknowledgments 11

Introduction 13

1. The Power in Choosing Strength 19

2. Strong Women Understand Their Identity
   and Their Purpose 31

3. Strong Women Choose the Word over the World 43

4. Strong Women Go to the Ball 55

5. Strong Women Maximize Their Mental Real Estate ... 67

6. Strong Women Believe in Miracles 79

7. Strong Women Use Their Words Wisely 91

8. Strong Women Say Yes, No, or Nothing at All 101

9. Strong Women Listen 111

10. Strong Women Use Their Strengths to Succeed 123

11. Strong Women Pursue a Clear Vision for
    Their Lives 137

12. Strong Women Forgive 149

13. Strong Women Know When to Move On 157

14. Strong Women Bounce Back 167

15. Strong Women Pray 177

16. Strong Women Give 187

17. Strong Women Choose Faith over Fear 199

18. Strong Women Guard Their Soul 211

19. Strong Women Finish Powerfully 221

Conclusion 229

Spiritual Strength Training:
  Questions and Action Steps for Each Chapter 231

Appendix: Strong Woman, It's Time to Thrive 242

Notes 252

About the Author 256

ACKNOWLEDGMENTS

Dr. Jeff Ogle: Thank you for collaborating with me on this book. I am beyond grateful for the tireless work you put into bringing it to life. The long hours were made easier with your help. I can't thank you enough.

Alyssa LaCourse: Thank you for being my agent! Your encouragement has been so helpful. Thank you for being on my team.

Melissa Lee: My dear friend and cohost, thank you for inspiring me with your encouragement, laughter, and kindness. You always bring fun to every project.

I want to give a special thanks to those who endorsed this book. It means the world to me. I am so excited to be able to build up godly women of faith, and I thank God for the opportunity to bring hope and joy in Jesus into the world.

Kim Jones, aka Real Talk Kim   Duane and Francie Chapman
April Osteen Simons   Kate McVeigh
Lisa Osteen Comes   Joni Lamb
Melissa Lee   Terri Savelle Foy
Tim Storey

To my other sweet friends who helped me bring this book to life, Elizabeth Lee and Gary-Robert Lee, thank you for your time and dedication. I am so blessed to have you in my corner. Thank you for supporting me through this process.

A special thank you to Lois Puglisi for your time and effort in making sure women get the opportunity to discover their true strength. I appreciate all you've done.

INTRODUCTION

When I wrote the book *Discover Your True Worth*, it had such a freeing feeling to it. Finding out we have value can take us to places that perhaps we never thought we could go. I've lived long enough to see the value and worth the world places on humanity, particularly on women. In some ways, the world ascribes great value to women. In other ways, the world devalues and even disdains them. That is why discovering our *true* worth and value in Christ is so important.

When we realize the value God places on us, it can lead us to make important decisions for our lives and futures. It can empower us to follow our hearts in ways we've never followed them before. It can give us the confidence we need to take the steps of faith God calls us to take. And it can lead us to discover and live from the strength God desires us to experience.

I've written *Discover Your True Strength* to help you on the journey of the rest of your life. I hope and pray it will position you for fulfillment and success by helping you realize that, in Christ, you are stronger and more powerful than you may think. As you come to recognize and understand the strength that is in you, you can live each day to the fullest, doing what you love and are called to do. I pray this book will even help you find the *true strength* to do something so powerful that it will not only fulfill you, but it will also bless others—who can then find deep satisfaction and strength for themselves.

Each chapter of this book is designed to make you think and respond. James 2:20 teaches us that "*faith without good deeds* ["*works*" NKJV] *is useless*" (NLT)—meaning we must take action as an expression of our faith. So, each chapter endeavors to offer insight into a certain area of your life; awaken your mind, will, and emotions; and stir your spirit into becoming the most fulfilled "you" that you can be.

As you read about the experiences of strong women—in the Bible, throughout history, or in contemporary life—you can catch a glimpse of how they think and believe, and you can glean from their wisdom. You can see how strong women act, respond, listen, and speak—or choose to remain silent. You can learn how women of great substance and strength thrive, work smart, and give to others. You can also see how strong women make an exit when they need to leave certain situations behind, and how they act like a lady and hold their peace. My prayer is that you discover a host of other godly strengths and characteristics that have waltzed women into places of freedom they never believed possible.

It's my hope that as you read, study, and learn from the stories and truths in this book, God will allow the words to mentor you and guide you into a place where you become convinced that within you is the God-given strength to live a life of great impact for Him.

Throughout this book, when I talk about strength, I am referring to what I call *true* strength—to godly, biblical inner strength. Later in this introduction, I share three Scriptures that highlight what I mean. In my many years of ministry, I have found that women with inner strength, the kind that only knowing God can bring, react differently than women who don't operate from that same kind of strength. As a general observation, they act differently in the marketplace, with their families, the way they give, and the way they respond to unexpected circumstances. This book is filled with concepts and thoughts coming from my encounters with strong women of Christian faith who walk in the strength and glory of Jesus Christ as their Lord.

When I was young, I remember people talking about situations or circumstances changing "in a snap." They would count to three and then snap their fingers as if things could or would change that quickly—for good or for bad. Or, they would use a phrase like "in the twinkling of an eye" while snapping their fingers. As a young child, I never really knew what that meant. But now, as an adult, I get it. I've come to understand how quickly things *can* change.

Lasting change, however, usually takes time and practice. The cartoon character Popeye could quickly consume a can of spinach, and immediately, big rippling muscles would appear on his arms. But the people I've encountered develop strength slowly. Becoming stronger is a process that happens over days, weeks, months, and years. My prayer is that you will begin to see yourself as an amazing, capable, more-than-able-to-do-what-it-takes kind of woman—that you will discover your *true* strength and see yourself as strong enough to do what God has planned for you, strong enough to do what is necessary for your amazing success in life. Then I believe everything else can fall into place. I call this "living from the inside out."

That's why, throughout this book, I want you to think about the possibilities God makes available to you. Things may change for you quickly, but, more often, growth and change take place over time. I encourage you to be patient with yourself.

Jesus says that we do not live "*by bread alone, but by every word that proceeds from the mouth of God*" (Matthew 4:4). Bread is great, but bread alone only provides natural sustenance. To live a supernatural life and have supernatural strength, we need the Word of God. Another reason I wrote this book is so you can grow in your knowledge of God's Word to help you live a successful, blessed, joyful life and eventually encourage others to do the same. God has ordained a path through life for you—a life-giving path of strength and success, filled with victory and joy—and it's in His Word.

This book is built on a foundation of three Scriptures: Ephesians 6:10, Philippians 4:13, and Nehemiah 8:10. As you begin the journey toward greater strength in Him, I hope you'll keep these three Scriptures in mind. I encourage you to meditate on them and to begin to see yourself operating in the strength of the Word of God. No matter what situation you're facing, I hope these Scriptures will help you to believe that *"with God all things are possible"* (Matthew 19:26). Let's take a quick look at these verses.

1. *"Be strong in the Lord and in the power of His might"* (Ephesians 6:10).

I love this Scripture so much because it says that we can be strong in the Lord—not just in our own power. We can be strong *in the Lord* and in the power of *His* might. First, we recognize that He is Lord, and then we acknowledge that He has great might. Ephesians 3:20–21 says that God has power. I have to remind myself that the pressure's off; I don't have to have mighty power. I just have to connect to the One who does, and you can connect to that power too.

2. *"I can do all things through Christ who strengthens me"* (Philippians 4:13).

Once we realize that, by faith, we can connect to the One who is all-powerful, almighty, all strength, we can put that strength to good use and believe we can do everything God has called us to do.

3. *"The joy of the Lord is your strength"* (Nehemiah 8:10).

When we can connect with the strength that God makes available to us, we are able to do what we're called to do, and we can live in a continuous state of joy.

To live in a state of joy doesn't mean giggling our way through each day. Not everything is funny, happy, or joyful in and of itself. But this Scripture clearly refers to the joy of the Lord. This is a joy we experience through the power and presence of God Himself. The amazing thing about this verse is that once we get a hold of it, we truly can live in a state of joy, the joy of the Lord.

Circumstances, relational issues, financial stress, conflicts over politics, trouble at work, and other negative situations can come and go in our life. Even people can come and go in life. But one thing that is constant forever is that the joy of the Lord is our strength. Every day, we can approach each situation with joy through the joy of the Lord, and this puts us in a position of strength.

God would not have included these Scriptures in the Bible if He didn't intend for us to live by them and for them to benefit us. So, I encourage you to dive into this book with anticipation and take the exciting, miraculous journey of discovering and living from your *true* strength.

SOMETIMES LIFE DEMANDS
THAT WE GO FROM ONE LEVEL
OF STRENGTH TO THE NEXT. I
BELIEVE WE ARE LIVING IN A
DAY WHEN, AS WOMEN OF GOD,
OUR STRENGTH IS NEEDED
MORE THAN EVER. I ALSO
BELIEVE THAT WITH GOD, WE
CAN BE STRONGER THAN WE
ALREADY ARE.

1

THE POWER IN CHOOSING STRENGTH

Do not strive in your own strength; cast yourself at the feet
of the Lord Jesus, and wait upon Him in the sure confidence
that He is with you, and works in you.
—Andrew Murray[1]

Sometimes life has a way of weakening people. It's peppered with what I call *strength-stealers*—situations, experiences, or relationships that cause us to feel like something has taken a vacuum cleaner to our courage, our fight, or our passion and sucked the strength out of us. Sometimes, they are disguised as the stresses and situations we face on a daily basis, and they can wear us down. Other times, they are so hidden in our regular routine that we can overlook them, allowing them to drain our strength drop by precious drop until we realize we are exhausted. Unless we deliberately choose to stand strong in the face of strength-stealers, they can deplete us.

As you read this book, my prayer is that you find its pages to be filled with encouraging words of hope and God-given strength. As we address the strength-stealers of your life, I want to remind you that God can restore anything that we lay at his feet. Through the younger years of my life, I walked around with these strength-stealers weighing me down, but because I received the good news of the gospel, I was set free. The purpose of this book is for you to be set free in every area of your life so that you can experience God's peace, love, and joy on a daily basis, regardless of your circumstances.

I'll share one of my big strength-stealers shortly. But, before I do, I want you to consider some of the possible strength-stealers in your life, such as:

+ Unexpected financial pressure
+ The pain of watching a son or daughter struggle in life
+ An unwanted divorce
+ An unforeseen accident
+ A chronic illness
+ An unintended addiction
+ A devastating loss
+ A daunting task
+ A great joy that somehow turned into sorrow
+ A fabulous job that became uncomfortable unemployment

The list goes on. Every woman I have ever known has had at least one strength-stealer in her life—and usually more than one. She's had something to overcome or work through, some metaphoric giant to slay in order to discover her *true* strength. For me, part of finding my *true* strength meant believing I would have children when doctors were certain I wouldn't—after suffering miscarriages and enduring surgeries, then losing a newborn son just hours after his long-awaited birth. These experiences could have weakened me, but with God's help and supportive family and friends, they ultimately developed in me a strength of compassion I never could have had otherwise to help women in similar circumstances. They also strengthened my faith to continue trusting God against great odds for the children He wanted me to have—three beautiful daughters who bring joy to my heart every day. The loss of our first child intensified my love and gratitude for the children God eventually gave to my husband, Richard, and me.

Was the journey through infertility and loss grueling? Yes, it was agony. I don't believe for a minute that God caused it, but I do believe He used it to strengthen me. I am keenly aware that some women face the same circumstances I faced—longing for biological children yet repeatedly being disappointed and heartbroken. Every woman's journey does not end with the same outcome I ultimately experienced. If that is your situation, I pray for you even as I write these words. My heart goes out to you as only the heart of a fellow traveler can. So, I pray that God does something supernatural, something miraculous that is so amazing and so redemptive that it will leave you in awe of His power and His love.

Being unable to have children for years, suffering miscarriages, then losing the first child I carried to full term were strength-stealers for me for sure. Strength-stealers may have entered your life because of your gender or your culture. You may have been told you were weak, undesirable, or somehow less worthy than other people because of your appearance, your personality, your interests, your parentage or ethnicity, or simply because someone in your life wanted you to be different from the way you are. You may have been shamed and blamed for things you have no power to change. These situations can have an impact. They can affect us. But strength-stealers don't have to be permanent. You can become stronger than they are. Perhaps my personal experiences are the reason I'm so passionate about this book and this message of strength.

In the examples I have mentioned, I may not have highlighted anything that directly pertains to your life, but I suspect something specific comes to mind for you. Perhaps you've encountered a situation that has left you feeling like you simply don't have the desire to pursue your passions or your dreams. Maybe you're surviving, but you're not thriving. You want to, but you're not—not by a little or even by a long shot.

If this describes you, then you are the very person for whom I've written this book. The way I see it, any strength-stealer in any amount, big or small, is still a hindrance—and it really can be overcome with God's help. My prayer is that by the time you finish reading, you'll realize that God has made you much stronger than you may think and that you will be equipped to choose strength in every situation. I'm not implying in any way that you aren't currently strong. You are probably stronger than I can imagine and perhaps stronger than *you* can even imagine. But sometimes life demands that we go from one level of strength to the next. I believe we are living in a day when, as women of God, our strength is needed more than ever. I also believe that with God, we can be stronger than we already are.

STRENGTH ON THE INSIDE

The word *strength* carries different meanings in different contexts. It can refer to physical might, or to bodybuilders' bulk, or to intellectual or persuasive ability, such as "a strong argument." It may relate to creativity, as in "a strong idea." It may describe the closeness of a bond between two people, as in the case of "a strong relationship." It can characterize effectiveness, like "strong leadership." It can even cause us to think of natural elements, such as mountains, or constructed elements, such as the foundation of a building.

In this book, we'll focus on strength in terms of inner fortitude, or spiritual power on the inside. We're talking about trusting

God for the ability to stand firm and confident in the face of life's difficulties and being able to remain peaceful and composed when life's storms come our way. This is the type of strength and stability that makes people wonder where you got it from. Ephesians 6:10 teaches us that we can *"be strong in the Lord and in the power of His might."* The strength that comes from God is available to us every moment of every day.

> THE *TRUE* STRENGTH I AM REFERRING TO
> IS FOUND IN CHOOSING GOD'S WORD AND
> BELIEVING IT IS FOR YOU ON A
> CONTINUAL BASIS.

Since strength is available, you may ask, "Why don't I feel strong?" or, "Why do certain things seem to get me down or set me back?" I believe the answer is simple: the *true* strength I am referring to is found in choosing God's word and believing it is for you on a continual basis. It's not a quality you're born with or something you study in school. I believe it's an option where you can decide whether or not you want it. There will be situations to deal with in life—the good, the bad, and everything in between. It's not just the circumstances themselves, but our responses to them, that matter. If you decide to choose the strength and power of God that reside in you, I believe you'll be glad you did. It can make for a life in which you can say to God, "We've got this!"

CHOOSE STRENGTH

You may remember Joshua in the Bible. He's the one who led the Israelites into the promised land after Moses finished his course and died in the wilderness. It was an intimidating assignment because, among other challenges, there were giants in that land, and they would have to be dealt with. Please read carefully what God said to Joshua as he prepared for battle:

After the death of Moses the servant of the LORD, it came to pass that the LORD spoke to Joshua the son of Nun, Moses' assistant, saying: "Moses My servant is dead. Now therefore, arise, go over this Jordan, you and all this people, to the land which I am giving to them—the children of Israel. Every place that the sole of your foot will tread upon I have given you, as I said to Moses. From the wilderness and this Lebanon as far as the great river, the River Euphrates, all the land of the Hittites, and to the Great Sea toward the going down of the sun, shall be your territory. No man shall be able to stand before you all the days of your life; as I was with Moses, so I will be with you. I will not leave you nor forsake you. Be strong and of good courage, for to this people you shall divide as an inheritance the land which I swore to their fathers to give them. Only be strong and very courageous, that you may observe to do according to all the law which Moses My servant commanded you; do not turn from it to the right hand or to the left, that you may prosper wherever you go. This Book of the Law shall not depart from your mouth, but you shall meditate in it day and night, that you may observe to do according to all that is written in it. For then you will make your way prosperous, and then you will have good success. Have I not commanded you? Be strong and of good courage; do not be afraid, nor be dismayed, for the LORD your God is with you wherever you go." (Joshua 1:1–9)

Look again at verse 7—"*Only be strong and very courageous*"— and notice that God communicates a similar message again in verse 9: "*Be strong and of good courage; do not be afraid, nor be dismayed.*" God basically tells Joshua to choose strength, and He tells him why he can count on it: because "*the LORD your God is with you wherever you go.*"

While all of Scripture is divinely inspired and important, I always pay extra attention when the Bible repeats a concept. God made sure "be strong" was repeated. Because of what God had called Joshua to do (to lead His people into the promised land after forty long years of wandering in the wilderness), and because He knew Joshua, He must have known Joshua could be intimidated by the battle ahead of him. Because God wanted Joshua to succeed, He repeated the instruction to be strong and courageous. He wanted Joshua to *choose* strength.

You may not be called to lead an entire nation in battle, as Joshua was, but I believe God has called you to do something important in His eyes. It may be to help guide a toddler or to help a young girl learn to value herself and celebrate her uniqueness. It may be to encourage your spouse, provide practical assistance to aging parents, or pour your heart into your children as a single parent. It may be to use your exceptional ability to handle challenges or to be resilient in the face of setbacks. It could be to dance or sing or draw or paint. It may be to take over a family business, start your own business, or rise to a new level of leadership in your profession. It may be to learn to set healthy boundaries and begin to build better relationships. Whatever God has called you to do, I pray for you to be strong and courageous to do it.

The Bible sometimes uses the words "take courage" or "took courage." They're not used in Joshua's story, but they are used in the story of the good king Asa, who eradicated idol worship among God's people and restored the worship of God. According to 2 Chronicles 15:8:

> *And when Asa heard these words and the prophecy of Oded the prophet, he took courage, and removed the abominable idols from all the land of Judah and Benjamin and from the cities which he had taken in the mountains of Ephraim; and*

he restored the altar of the LORD that was before the vestibule of the LORD.

And Psalm 31:24 instructs us: *"Be strong, and let your heart take courage, all you who wait for the LORD!"* (ESV).

I like the phrase *"take courage"* because, again, it tells me that courage is available and can be mine for the taking. God provides it, and I can choose to take hold of it or to let it pass me by. It's not a passive quality that will simply show up in my life; I believe we have to take an active role in taking courage for ourselves, with God's help.

This directive was important for Joshua, and I believe it's important for you and me. Joshua had a choice to make, and so do we. He chose strength—and he fulfilled not only God's plan for His life, but also God's purposes for an entire nation.

I think Joshua came to understand the power of choice, because he tells the Israelites in Joshua 24:15, *"Choose for yourselves this day whom you will serve."* He goes on to say, *"But as for me and my house, we will serve the LORD."* He made his choice, and, as best we can tell from Scripture, he never wavered from it.

> WHATEVER GOD HAS CALLED YOU TO DO,
> I PRAY FOR YOU TO BE STRONG AND
> COURAGEOUS TO DO IT.

God gives all of us free will. He lets us choose what we will do or won't do, what we will think or won't think, what we will say or won't say. He leads us and guides us by His Spirit, and I believe He rejoices when we choose correctly. But He never forces us to make good choices. That's up to us.

Choosing strength is what I call a "DIYD"—a do-it-yourself decision. It's personal. You may need encouragement or help along the way, and I would encourage you to get all the help you need from the trustworthy people and places you can find it. And, since you're the one who can make the commitment and the investment in it, the good news is that you're the one who will reap the rewards.

> I BELIEVE WE HAVE TO TAKE AN ACTIVE ROLE
> IN TAKING COURAGE FOR OURSELVES,
> WITH GOD'S HELP.

SOME CHOICES OF THE STRONG

Discovering your true strength, your godly strength, can start with a single choice to receive the strength only God can give you (Ephesians 6:10). But that's not the only choice you will ever need to make. Consider embracing some of the choices I have watched strong, godly women make as they chose:

- Forgiveness over holding grudges
- Peace over anger
- Faith over fear
- Love over hate
- Freedom over bondage
- Finishing over quitting
- Being agreeable over being displeasing
- Wisdom over foolishness
- Trust over worry
- Belief over doubt
- Hope over hopelessness
- Gratitude over thanklessness
- Giving over not giving

- Building people up over putting them down
- The Word of God over the ways of the world
- Humility over pretentiousness
- Unity over division
- Truth over lies, deception, or "spin"
- Discipline over laziness
- The joy of the Lord over lack of joy

Notice that the choices listed above fall into the realm of the soul, our inner man that follows the instruction of the Lord through His Word. My preferred definition of "soul" is that it is composed of our mind, our will, and our emotions. As I mentioned earlier, for the purpose of this book, we are using the word *strong* as it relates to strength on the inside—the strength of our inner man, which comes from the Lord.

Think about your soul as being like the square footage of a house. We all have a certain amount of what I call real estate in our soul. We let various things occupy the space in our minds (thoughts) and in our wills (choices) and in our emotions (feelings). I know that from time to time, I allow the wrong things to fill my soul. But it doesn't have to be that way. We can all decide to feed our souls with what is positive and godly rather than what is negative and worldly. When we make that decision and stick with it, scriptural change begins to happen. Is it all instantly perfect? I don't think so. But the best way I know to get to the finish line is to start somewhere.

START WITH ONE CHOICE

I often say that the only way to count to one million is to start with one. The journey of a thousand steps starts the first time you put one foot in front of the other. Just as the process of becoming physically stronger can begin with picking up the first weight, the process of becoming stronger on the inside starts with taking hold of the truth that you can be strong in the Lord and committing by faith to becoming stronger than perhaps you ever imagined. Remember, *"the joy of the* LORD *is your strength"* (Nehemiah 8:10). The journey to greater strength may require making some challenging choices, but I believe it can also be filled with great joy.

SUMMARY

1. Be on guard against the strength-stealers in your life, the daily situations that can wear you down and deplete you of faith and joy. Stand against them in the power of God's Word.

2. God has made you much stronger than perhaps you think you are. His Word says to "be strong" and "take courage." This biblical strength, given to us by God, is available to you at all times. But you have to choose to take hold of it. It won't happen automatically.

3. I believe that God has something important for every believer to do, and, because of that, He has given you the power and strength you need to fulfill His purpose for your life. Whatever God has called you to do, I encourage you to be strong and courageous and do it (1 Chronicles 28:20).

4. Discovering your true strength may start with one choice, like choosing to receive the strength that only God can give, but it continues as you make thousands of other choices in your life. Once you decide to feed your soul with the positive and godly rather than the negative and worldly, change can begin to happen.

NOTES TO SELF

Now that you've read this chapter, what notes would you like to write to yourself to help you remember the strength-building points that are most helpful to you or that apply to a specific situation in your life?

____

____

____

____

____

2

STRONG WOMEN UNDERSTAND THEIR IDENTITY AND THEIR PURPOSE

I will praise You, for I am fearfully and wonderfully made;
marvelous are Your works,
and that my soul knows very well.
—Psalm 139:14

Many people today are searching to find out more and more about their identity—meaning, simply, who they are. Some do this by submitting DNA samples to groups that research their ancestry. They want to know where their family originated, hoping that will help them understand some of the characteristics, values, or desires they have.

Many people who delve into their ancestry have discovered relatives they never knew they had. Sometimes this turns out well for them, and sometimes it leads them to people they wish they had not found. Sometimes it yields positive experiences, and sometimes it brings challenges.

The identity-seeking business has become so popular that there are even ways people can investigate the backgrounds of their pets. These tests help owners understand their pets' traits and temperaments, along with providing information about their parents and siblings.

According to an article from *Business Insider*, "Genealogy research is a booming business."[1] This tells me that people are longing to know who they are and where they come from. It seems to me that they want to understand themselves and discover their true identity. And, while I'm not against searching out genic identity, I also pray that people can discover and understand their true biblical identity. Genesis 1:27 says God created us in His image. He designed us with a purpose. And my desire is to see us learn all we need to know about ourselves in the context of relationship with Him and His Word.

FEARFULLY AND WONDERFULLY MADE

Understanding your God-given identity can boost your self-awareness and self-esteem, and it can give you confidence. As you read at the beginning of this chapter, David writes in Psalm 139:14 that he praises God because he is *"fearfully and wonderfully made."* I believe this is true for each of us, and when we recognize it, it can change the way we view and think about ourselves.

Our enemy, the devil, works to steal the truth of God's Word from us so we will not apply it to our lives and live in its power. So, I have a question for you: Who are you listening to? For me, I had listened to the negative thoughts trying to steal my God-given identity with words like:

+ "You're not good enough."

+ "You're not qualified."

+ "You'll never be accepted."

- "You can't change."
- "You will always fail."

I had to lean on God's Word to overcome that way of thinking. If the devil is sending such accusing and discouraging messages to you, then I believe it is vitally important for you to know who you are in God. You can begin to come against those lies of the devil with truths about who God has created you to be, according to His Word, so you can speak them about yourself, starting with:

- "I am strong and courageous. I will not fear or be dismayed, for the Lord my God is with me wherever I go" (adapted from Joshua 1:9).
- "God loves me with an everlasting love. He draws me with lovingkindness" (adapted from Jeremiah 31:3).
- "Because I am in Christ, I am a new creation. I have been made new" (adapted from 2 Corinthians 5:17).
- "God chose me before the foundation of the world, that I should be holy and blameless before Him in love" (adapted from Ephesians 1:4).
- "I am God's workmanship, created in Christ Jesus for good works, and I will walk in them" (adapted from Ephesians 2:10).

I find that the way to become established in your godly identity is to read and study what His Word says about you. These Scriptures provide a good foundation, but as you do your own study, I believe you'll find many more encouraging truths in God's Word about who you are in Him.

IDENTITY COMES BEFORE IMPACT

I have read and studied God's Word for many years, and I have increasingly realized that Jesus is not just someone I've studied about in the Bible. The longer I walk with God and stay in His Word, the more I see that by God's power working in me, I am being transformed by Him to reflect my Savior more and more each day. In this way, I have found my *true* self and therefore found my *true* strength. I believe the same can happen for anyone who seeks to know who they are in Christ.

Second Corinthians 3:16–18 speaks of the transformation God works in our lives:

> *Nevertheless when one turns to the Lord, the veil is taken away. Now the Lord is the Spirit; and where the Spirit of the Lord is, there is liberty. But we all, with unveiled face, beholding as in a mirror the glory of the Lord, are being transformed into the same image from glory to glory, just as by the Spirit of the Lord.*

The better I understand and live from my identity in Christ, the better prepared I am to fulfill His purpose for my life—meaning, doing what He has called me to do. Jesus says, *"Most assuredly, I say to you, he who believes in Me, the works that I do he will do also; and greater works than these he will do, because I go to My Father"* (John 14:12). This verse gives the impression that Jesus has some impactful things for you and me to do. Wouldn't you agree? But before we skip over to the "doing," let's make sure we understand the importance of finding our identity in Christ.

I have found that who you are in Christ is more important than what you do. Once you know who you are in Him, you can more effectively figure out what to do. Again, identity comes before doing. Why? Because when you find your identity in Christ, your life can be transformed by Jesus, and He can give you His plan for your life. He can also give you His power through the Holy Spirit to live your life successfully and with great impact.

Jesus addressed this thought in Luke 10:17–24. He sent out seventy-two of His disciples to minister to people, and they returned rejoicing, telling Jesus that *even the demons are subject to us in Your name"* (verse 17). But Jesus cautioned them to rejoice in who they were (their identity), not in what they did (their activity). This is so important to understand because what you do can change. Where you go can also change, but who you are in Christ should not change. First John 4:4 says, *"You are of God, little children."* Because this identity comes from the Word of God, it is not meant to change—ever.

Colossians 1:24–29 is another must-read passage about discovering who you are in Christ. Verse 27 says clearly, *"To them God has chosen to make known among the Gentiles the glorious riches of this mystery, which is Christ in you, the hope of glory"* (NIV). While the normal way to deal with situations in life seems to be to assess things that we see on the outside and then process them on the inside, Colossians 1:27 shows us that because of Christ in us, He can work through us from the inside out.

> I HAVE FOUND THAT WHO YOU ARE IN CHRIST IS MORE IMPORTANT THAN WHAT YOU DO.

IDENTITY, PURPOSE, AND CALLING ARE CONNECTED

Bible teacher Joyce Meyer often says, "Your *who* is not your *do*." In other words, what we do—the roles we play in life, the jobs we do, the responsibilities we fulfill—do not define who we are.

While who we are is separate from what we do, it's also true that our identity is often connected to our purpose and calling. God creates us for a purpose, and He chooses various aspects of our nature to help us fulfill that purpose. Let's consider several

Bible stories about people whose callings helped them realize their identity.

MOSES

Moses did not fully know who he was until he met God at a burning bush and discovered that he was the one chosen to deliver God's people and bring six hundred thousand Israelite men, plus women and children, out of Egyptian bondage (Exodus 3; 12:37). Through his encounter with God, Moses discovered his true purpose.

DAVID

David was just a shepherd boy taking food to his brothers at the army encampment when he saw the giant Goliath and felt the anointing (grace and enablement) of God come upon him. There, he discovered he could defeat the giant with only a perfectly aimed, smooth stone from a slingshot (1 Samuel 17). I see this as the beginning of David understanding his purpose—to be a mighty king of God's people for forty years.

MARY, THE MOTHER OF JESUS

Mary was just a teenager who perhaps did not know who she was called to be until the angel Gabriel came to her and said, "*Rejoice, highly favored one, the Lord is with you; blessed are you among women!... And behold, you will conceive in your womb and bring forth a Son, and shall call His name Jesus*" (Luke 1:28, 31). Mary discovered her true godly purpose as the human vessel though which God would send His Son to earth to be the Savior of the world.

Moses, David, and Mary all had an identity apart from their callings. Inside each of them was a God-given desire to know, love, and serve the Lord. They trusted Him completely, and this is one reason He used them so mightily.

You may not be called to part the Red Sea and lead a nation into freedom like Moses was; or to go into battle for his nation, like

David was; or to have an assignment that is anything like Mary was given. But I believe you are called to be *you*. You are fearfully and wonderfully made (Psalm 139:13–14) *in order* to do all God has called you to do. The Bible teaches us that when God wants to use someone to fulfill a purpose, He looks for obedience perhaps more than He looks for certain other qualifications. I think it's very simple to understand that God does not always call the equipped—but He always equips the called.

"AH, LORD GOD!"

I love the book of Jeremiah. To me, the prophet Jeremiah has such a big personality. Take a look at a conversation he has with the Lord:

> *Then the word of the LORD came to me, saying: "Before I formed you in the womb I knew you; before you were born I sanctified you; I ordained you a prophet to the nations." Then said I: "Ah, Lord GOD! Behold, I cannot speak, for I am a youth." But the LORD said to me: "Do not say, 'I am a youth,' for you shall go to all to whom I send you, and whatever I command you, you shall speak. Do not be afraid of their faces, for I am with you to deliver you," says the LORD. Then the LORD put forth His hand and touched my mouth, and the LORD said to me: "Behold, I have put My words in your mouth. See, I have this day set you over the nations and over the kingdoms, to root out and to pull down, to destroy and to throw down, to build and to plant."* (Jeremiah 1:4–10)

I giggle when I read, "*Ah, Lord GOD!*" (verse 6). To me, it's as if Jeremiah is saying, "Oh, Lord, help me!" He reminds God that he is but a youth. He makes any excuse he can think of to try to get out of doing what God asked him to do. Finally, God gives Jeremiah a sweet pep talk, basically saying, "Don't panic when you see '*their faces.*'" God goes on to make it clear that He is the One who will really be doing the talking, the metaphoric heavy lifting—not Jeremiah. With that, Jeremiah is convinced and must have thought, "Whew!" The rest is biblical history.

Once Jeremiah heard God speak about his true identity (verse 5), he could understand and embrace his purpose. After this conversation, he obeyed God and went on to do great things for the Lord. Jeremiah knew who he was, but he also knew who God was—and that's where he kept his focus.

> WHEN WE KNOW WHO WE ARE AND WHAT
> GOD HAS CALLED US TO DO, WE CAN CONNECT
> WITH A SENSE OF WORTH—OUR WORTH TO GOD,
> TO OTHER PEOPLE, AND TO OURSELVES—AND
> REALIZE THAT WE ARE UNIQUE AND PRECIOUS.

YOU ARE VALUABLE

As we study the Bible and begin to realize our identity and purpose, we can understand our value as well. When we know who we are and what God has called us to do, we can connect with a sense of worth—our worth to God, to other people, and to ourselves—and realize that we are unique and precious.

I recently looked online to find the price of a football. A local sporting goods store was selling it for about $17.00. In my hands, it's worth just that: $17.00. But in former quarterback Tom Brady's hands, a football has been worth as much as fifteen million dollars.

I also looked online for the price of a sleeve of golf balls. They cost about $12.00. In my hands, they would be worth about $12.00. But in champion golfer Jordan Spieth's hands, they were worth close to thirty million dollars in 2023 alone.

I discovered that a baseball costs about $20.00 if ordered online. In my hands, a baseball would be worth only $20.00. But in the hands of World Series championship pitcher Justin Verlander, as of this writing, a baseball is worth more than forty million dollars per year.

I found that a professional tennis racket costs around $400.00 if ordered online. In my hands, the racket would be worth $400.00. But in tennis star Serena Williams's hands, a tennis racket was worth more than $45 million in 2021.

Finally, I looked for the price of three railroad spikes. They sell for about $3.75 each, making the total cost $11.25. But for similar spikes, when pierced through the hands and feet of Jesus as He was nailed to the cross two thousand years ago, the value was priceless because Jesus's crucifixion purchased our salvation and healing. And because Jesus went to the cross, our *true* identity, our *true* value, and our *true* strength becomes immeasurable.

So, the next time Satan tries to tell you that you have no value or no worth, remind him that the price Jesus paid for you was immeasurable. Nothing has ever been—or will ever be—so valuable to God as a human being, and that includes you and me.

GIVE WHAT YOU RECEIVE

I pray that this chapter has helped you find your *true* identity in Christ. As the reality of your *true* identity in Him continues to unfold, I believe you will experience His love, His compassion, and His power in increasing measure. It is my prayer that by the time you finish this book, you are ready to follow the instructions of Matthew 10:8: *"Freely you have received, freely give."* As you move forward with confidence in your identity in Christ, I pray that you will become empowered to share your new freedom and boldness with those around you.

SUMMARY

1. People long to know who they are and where they come from. But true, godly identity and purpose can only be fulfilled through a relationship with God and His Word, through knowing God's Son, Jesus Christ. As you understand and live from this God-given identity, you can be better prepared to do what He has called you to do.

2. I have found that knowing who you are in Christ is more important than anything you do. Discovering what to do with your life is certainly important, but to me, it's even more important to find your identity in Christ. Once you know who you are in Him, you can more effectively figure out what to do as you fulfill His plan for your life. Identity is often connected to purpose, as we read about in the stories of many Bible characters, such as Moses; David; Mary, the mother of Jesus; and Jeremiah.

3. Understanding your identity and purpose can help you understand your value or worth. While a football or a golf ball isn't exceptionally valuable on its own, in the hands of an elite athlete, it can be worth millions. And while this has great merit, according to the Bible, our true godly value should come from the One who created us. Jesus paid an incalculable price for you, and He called you His own.

4. Your identity and purpose are designed for godly impact when you live in the blessing of God. God has freely given to you, so I encourage you to find opportunities to share with others.

NOTES TO SELF

Now that you've read this chapter, what notes would you like to write to yourself to help you remember the strength-building points that are most helpful to you or that apply to a specific situation in your life?

NO MATTER WHAT'S GOING
ON IN YOUR LIFE OR IN THE
WORLD, YOU CAN FACE IT
WITHOUT FEAR BECAUSE THE
BIBLE SAYS THAT GOD IS WITH
YOU, AND HE IS FOR YOU.

3

STRONG WOMEN CHOOSE THE WORD OVER THE WORLD

Do not be conformed to this world, but be transformed by the
renewal of your mind, that by testing you may discern what
is the will of God, what is good and acceptable and perfect.
—Romans 12:2 (ESV)

The world has its view of strength, and we see it everywhere we look. But God's Word also has a view of strength, and, for believers, it defines what true strength is—being strong in the Lord and in the power of His might (Ephesians 6:10). For example, the world says, "Do your own thing." The Word says, *"Do to others what you would have them do to you"* (Matthew 7:12 NIV). The world says, "You have to maneuver and do certain things to get ahead." The Word says, *"A person's gift makes room for him and brings him before great people"* (Proverbs 18:16 NASB). I say, those who live by the Word, while navigating through the world, have an amazing opportunity to find true strength.

I probably don't have to tell you that the world we live in is changing rapidly. Maybe change is happening in your life or in your family's life, and it's left you feeling that you don't know what to do. Maybe you do know what to do but lack the strength and confidence to do it. Maybe you find the situation in the world around us disorienting, even disturbing. Or perhaps you know you need greater strength for the days ahead, but you aren't sure how to get it. It's my desire for you to see God as the strength you need for whatever circumstances you may face.

No matter what's going on in your life or in the world, you can face it without fear because the Bible says that God is with you, and He is for you. He is strong and mighty (Ephesians 6:10). You can do all things through Christ who strengthens you (Philippians 4:13). And because you are in Christ, you can go through it all stronger and more joyful than you ever thought possible.

DROP THE *L*

While the world can change rapidly, and change can bring confusion, there is a consistency we can depend on—God. God doesn't bring confusion, nor does His Word. He says in Malachi 3:6, "*I the* LORD *do not change*" (ESV). And Hebrews 13:8 declares, "*Jesus Christ is the same yesterday, today, and forever.*" Look at the simple difference between the spelling of the word *word* and the word *world*. The only difference is one letter: the letter *l*. Most of the information we receive from the media—whether from television, the Internet, or other sources—may come from the *world's point of view*, not always from the perspective of *God's Word*. The world's point of view can often be summarized by the term *existentialism*, which is the approach emphasizing the existence of a person who chooses to determine their own development through acts of the will only.[1] For me, I see this as forming opinions and facing decisions without referencing the Word of God.

Sometimes what the world says can be opposite of what the Word says. We live in the world, but we are not *of* the world (John 17:14–15). First John 4:4 says we are "*of God*" and teaches us that Jesus, who lives in us, is "*greater than he who is in the world.*" This means that living by the Word, as opposed to living according to the system of the world, allows us an opportunity to operate with a greater power than the world might offer.

In the world, we see fear, lack, jealousy, stress, jockeying for power, greed, and many other attitudes and behaviors that can make life strained or unhappy. In contrast, God's Word says we can live in peace (Romans 12:18), with our needs met (Philippians 4:19), loving and helping others (1 John 4:7), preferring others over ourselves (Romans 12:10), trusting God to protect and defend us (Psalm 91), and giving generously (2 Corinthians 9:11). As believers, we are to renew our minds, according to Romans 12:2, allowing the truths and principles of God's Word to supersede those of the world.

Matthew 6:33 tells us that when we seek first the kingdom of God and His righteousness, everything else we need *"shall be added"* to us. This word *shall* is interesting. I didn't choose it; I'm simply quoting it. The word *shall* is similar to the more modern word *will*. It's like God's guarantee. I've seen some guarantees in the world that hold true and some guarantees in the world that seem to vaporize into the wind. But for thousands of years, the Bible has had a track record of success. I believe when God says He will do something, He will do it. He may not do it immediately, but His timing will be as He sees fit, and He *will* make good on His Word. Because of His track record, I choose to believe the Word over the world. I pray you will too.

In John 16:33, Jesus said, *"In the world you will have tribulation; but be of good cheer, I have overcome the world."* I think this statement indicates that Jesus recognizes that the world has deficiencies, issues, and problems. However, remember that we are to be in the world but not *of* it. As believers, we have a right to see things through the lens of God.

As born-again believers, we are to live by God's Word, its teachings, and its ways. We are made new, spiritually speaking, in Christ (2 Corinthians 5:17). This means God's Spirit lives within us (Romans 8:9), and we can live as God wants us to live, following Jesus's example. We are God's children (John 1:12), His chosen ones (1 Peter 2:9), and we can live under the blessings of our Father. God wants to bless us and make us a blessing to others (2 Corinthians 9:8–11).

> AS BELIEVERS, WE HAVE A RIGHT TO SEE THINGS
> THROUGH THE LENS OF GOD.

THE TITLE DEED TO WHAT YOU NEED

Romans 1:17 says, *"The just shall live by faith."* Note that Hebrews 11:1 says faith is the substance of what we are hoping for. To me, it's my belief system coupled with the understanding that God will do what He says He will do. True biblical faith takes our ability to believe for something and lines it up with the Word and will of God.

If we look again at Hebrews 11:1, we see that faith is not only *"the substance of things hoped for,"* but it is also *"the evidence of things not seen."* Look at the word *"substance."* One of the *Amplified Bible*'s expanded terms for this word is *"title deed."* When we believe God's Word by faith, we can have the title deed to the blessings and good gifts God has for us. Let's choose the blessings of God's Word over the enticements of the world and remember Hebrews 11:6 says that *"God…is a rewarder of those who diligently seek Him."*

BLESSED

I find Deuteronomy to be one of the most fascinating books in the Bible. Chapter 28 clearly explains the possible outcome of our belief system and God's reward system. I think Deuteronomy 28:1–8 really comes alive in *The Message*:

> *If you listen obediently to the Voice of GOD, your God, and heartily obey all his commandments that I command you today, GOD, your God, will place you on high, high above all the nations of the world. All these blessings will come down on you and spread out beyond you because you have responded to the Voice of GOD, your God:*
>
> > *GOD's blessing inside the city,*
> >
> > *GOD's blessing in the country;*
> >
> > *GOD's blessing on your children,*
> >
> > > *the crops of your land,*
> > >
> > > *the young of your livestock,*
> > >
> > > *the calves of your herds,*
> > >
> > > *the lambs of your flocks.*
> >
> > *GOD's blessing on your basket and bread bowl;*
> >
> > *GOD's blessing in your coming in,*
> >
> > *GOD's blessing in your going out.*
>
> *GOD will defeat your enemies who attack you. They'll come at you on one road and run away on seven roads.*
>
> *GOD will order a blessing on your barns and workplaces; he'll bless you in the land that GOD, your God, is giving you.*

I think of this passage in terms of "voices and choices." As we hear things in the world, we can choose to agree with them or to disagree with them. We can choose to believe and agree with things that send us into fear, or we can choose to believe and agree with things that propel us into faith. But I believe the exciting thing is this: the choice is ours. Joshua 24:15 says, *"Choose for yourselves this day whom you will serve.*" In spite of all the information we have to process on a daily basis, we still have to make a conscious choice to serve the Lord, obey His Word, and live with the outcome.

WHAT'S IN YOUR BOX?

As a child, my daughter, Chloe, had the most unusual yet adorable box she referred to as her "treasure box." It contained everything that had great value to her. Recently, we found that box, and she and I sat on the floor pulling out each piece she had saved and laughing at its meaning or lack thereof. Much of what was in the box was so precious that, all these years later, it still has great value. However, some of it was unidentifiable junk.

Chloe's treasure box reminds me of life. Some things in our lives are to be treasured because they have great value. Some things don't belong in our lives, and some things are unidentifiable junk. Our challenge comes as we identify what's what and then decide what to do with it.

To make matters more complicated, we don't always get to choose what goes in the boxes of our lives. Sometimes we make poor choices and put something negative into our lives. And sometimes other people do things that are beyond our control.

THE "HELL" IN THE BOX

Years ago, I was ministering in a large church with an audience of thousands. I took a giant box with me in order to demonstrate the choices available to us as believers. I called the sermon "Get the Hell Out of My Box." I was using the word *hell* as a noun to identify it as Satan's dwelling place—not God's, and certainly not a Christian's. Furthermore, *Merriam-Webster.com* describes hell as "a situation or state that causes great suffering and unhappiness."[1]

If we can experience heaven on earth, I believe we can also experience hellish situations on earth.

If I find myself in a hellish situation, the first thing I do is pray for God to direct me. Then I can get busy figuring out how to get past it. In addition, I can make the choice to pray and command Satan's forces to get out of my life and take his plans with him.

GET THE "HELL" OUT OF YOUR LIFE

My husband, Richard, tells a story about his father, Oral Roberts. As a teenager, Richard was golfing one day with his father. His dad was trying to convince him to join the ministry and take a serious look at the choices he was making in his life and the outcomes those choices would create. The conversation eventually became uncomfortable. Richard reached the point where his dad had placed enough pressure on him that he said, "Dad, get the hell out of my life!"

Immediately and comically, Oral responded by saying, "Richard, that's what I'm trying to do. I'm trying to get the hell out of your life!" Message understood. Enough said. At the age of nineteen, Richard gave his heart to the Lord and joined the ministry, and he has been living a life filled with the Spirit of God ever since.

This is another example of "voices and choices." When Richard heard the voice of his earthly father, he reacted in a negative way. But when his earthly father explained what he thought the voice of the heavenly Father was saying and told Richard how his life could change for good, Richard chose to accept Jesus. From that moment on, he's had the opportunity to live in God's blessing. Has he always gotten everything right? No. He's human. However, he's had the opportunity to seek the things of God, to seek first the kingdom of God by living God's way, and he's been mightily blessed. When we choose the Word and all it represents over the world and all it represents, we can live in blessings we once only imagined.

> WHEN WE CHOOSE THE WORD AND ALL IT REPRESENTS OVER THE WORLD AND ALL IT REPRESENTS, WE CAN LIVE IN BLESSINGS WE ONCE ONLY IMAGINED.

"HELP! HELP! JANE, STOP THIS CRAZY THING!"

When I was a child, I watched a cartoon called *The Jetsons*. The Jetson family lived in the Skypad Apartments in Orbit City, where all the buildings extended from earth high into the atmosphere. The Jetsons enjoyed all the modern conveniences of a space-age lifestyle: flying cars, robotics, self-cleaning appliances, and more. Now, the comedy to me is that I've lived long enough to actually see a lot of the futuristic things the Jetsons owned become realities.

As the closing credits of the show roll, George takes the family dog, Astro, for a walk. But because they live up in the sky, he can't just walk out the door of the house. He walks the dog on a machine that looks like a treadmill. The cat jumps on the treadmill, the dog starts chasing the cat, and the machine speeds out of control. George loses his balance, becomes frantic, and screams for his wife, Jane, to come to his rescue. "Help! Help!" he cries out, "Jane, stop this crazy thing!"

Sometimes, George Jetson's situation reminds me of life. While I'm trying to get from one place to another and lots of things are happening, life can turn upside down in an instant. I don't even want to count how many times this has happened to me, my family, or our ministry. It was such a help for George to have Jane presumably standing nearby, able to rescue him. And just as

Jane was there to rescue George Jetson, I believe God is available to rescue and support us!

GOD WAS THERE

In the past, when life spun out of control for me, my family was always there to pray, support me, and offer practical help. Our ministry team was there to pray when I needed prayer. Often, I was able to reach out to a friend or a coworker. At all times, God was there, but I had to *recognize* that He was there. I had to stretch out my faith. I had to believe for the situation to be different. I had to exercise my voice and make a choice. Would I listen to the way of the world or follow the way of the Word? Again, we're back to voices and choices. Remembering Joshua 24:15, I had to decide that "as for me and my house, we will serve the Lord." I might not have seen an instant turnaround, but I knew God was always there and had miracle answers with my name on them.

I believe that as you choose the Word over the world in your life, you'll position yourself to see miracles too. I know there are a lot of pressures that go along with following the ways of the world. You may be in a situation at work, in your neighborhood or community, or in some other way where believing the Word makes you feel you're swimming upstream. I believe God can give you a clear direction as to how you can metaphorically swim anyway. That way, God is in the "stream" with you. As you choose to believe God's Word in the midst of the world you live in, I believe it's the best decision you'll ever make—and it can become the foundation of the strength you long for.

SUMMARY

1. There's only a one-letter difference between the words *world* and *Word*, but there's a huge difference in the outcome, depending on which one you follow. We live in the blessings of God's Word. We can choose to believe the Word and act on it.

2. Faith is the belief that God will do what He says He will do. When, by faith, we believe God's Word, we can have the title deed to every blessing and good gift God has prepared for us.

3. In life, we encounter many voices and choices. We can choose to believe the things of the world that can send us into fear, or we can choose the things of the Word that can propel us into faith. The exciting thing is this: we get to choose to be involved in the decision-making process. *"Choose for yourselves this day whom you will serve"* (Joshua 24:15).

4. Recognize that God is always there. Stretch out your faith, exercise your voice, and make a choice—to follow the Word, even though you are in the world.

NOTES TO SELF

Now that you've read this chapter, what notes would you like to write to yourself to help you remember the strength-building points that are most helpful to you or that apply to a specific situation in your life?

_____

_____

_____

_____

_____

ACHIEVING YOUR DREAMS,
GOALS, AND YOUR HAPPILY
EVER AFTER MAY OR MAY NOT
MEET WITH THE SUPPORT OF
THOSE AROUND YOU. BUT IF
IT'S SUPPORTED BY GOD, YOU
CAN GO TO THE BALL WITH
CONFIDENCE.

4

STRONG WOMEN GO TO THE BALL

God never said that the journey would be easy, but he did say that the arrival would be worthwhile.
—Max Lucado[1]

I wrote this chapter as a result of the story of a sweet friend of mine who allowed God to turn her tragedy into triumph and her devastation into the things dreams are made of. After losing her beloved husband to a horrible battle with cancer, she found herself without clear direction from God regarding her future. Much time passed, but her pain seemed to increase.

Her husband had been in business, and one of his clients called one day, looking for him. This caught her off guard. At first, the caller couldn't understand why she began to cry, and he apologized profusely. When she was finally able to explain that her husband had passed into heaven, he explained that he, too, had just experienced the loss of a spouse. After many long conversations, a time of healing, and much prayer, these two people married and are now both serving God in ministry. Their journey wasn't easy or without opposition. But the good news is that they found each other. I lovingly refer to my friend as Cinderella—God's example of "happily ever after."

THE PRINCESS AND THE QUEEN

Many people see the fairy tale of Cinderella as simply a beautiful love story with a happily-ever-after ending. The same can be said for Esther, the little orphan girl who ended up as a queen. Her story is found in the book of the Bible that bears her name. She lived *"for such a time as this"* (Esther 4:14), meaning she was born for a purpose, which she ultimately fulfilled.

I agree with these assessments of Cinderella and Esther, but let's focus on the fact that they decided to go to the ball, so to speak. By saying they "went to the ball," I mean they chose to take the necessary steps to accomplish what they were created to do— they acted.

Realistically speaking, how many of us have the opportunity to go to a royal ball and marry a prince (like Cinderella), or to go to a royal feast and marry a king (like Esther)? None of this could have happened to either of these women had they not made the important decision to go to the ball.

THE COMPANY YOU KEEP

Most of us live in the "real world," where we are often surrounded by other people. In Cinderella's fairy tale, certain people in the story could not be avoided—like her wicked stepmother and step-sisters. I know that some stepfamily members are amazing, but, in this fairy tale, our dear Cinderella had to endure inescapable cruelty. I believe that this type of thing happens to all of us, even if it is not exactly like Cinderella's experience. There are people in our lives that we simply can't avoid, no matter how they treat us or how much negativity they bring into our lives. Yet I have found that no matter how many metaphorical wicked-witch encounters

I have faced, God was always there, providing someone to get me out of the clutches of the evil that tried to steal my peace, joy, and God-given destiny. He put me in the path of strength-givers and helped me steer clear of strength-stealers.

My story was simple. I spent many years surrounded by books, words, and notes. I had a deep desire to be an excellent—and even perfect—student. To me, a test score of 98 percent was equal to failure. I had a hard time separating excellence from a lifestyle of perfection until God set me free from perfectionism. But until then, I did all I could to go to college, earn a degree, and eventually go to law school. That was a shining moment in my life, for certain.

However, when I chose to marry Richard, the son of a "famous" (I'm so not fond of that word for many reasons) healing evangelist, and embark on a new life in the ministry, I was not prepared for what a friend called "the punishment of fame." Life got a little more complicated, but there was also joy and fulfillment in walking out God's purpose for my life. I had gained some dear God-filled friends, but also a few enemies.

Over the next four years, I experienced multiple surgeries and two miscarriages. Finally, Richard and I had a son. Our sweet boy only lived for thirty-six hours and died in our arms. From the dearest people who encouraged me to those I call the devil's "special agents," I learned about persecution and pain the hard way— through the most difficult moments of my life.

During this time, I was dealt a quick and agonizing lesson about the company we keep. While I heard heartfelt comments such as "I'm praying for you" from thoughtful friends, I also experienced harsh comments. A person actually said to me, "I prayed for that baby to die, and God answered my prayers." When I heard that, it was as though someone took the breath out of my body. The only way I was able to recover was through the Word of God. I had to guard my soul and spirit by surrounding myself with godly, life-speaking people. I found out firsthand how important it is to have godly, positive, supportive people around me and how brutal it can be to have ungodly, negative, destructive people around me.

In the Bible and in life, there is often someone who is for you and someone who is against you. Similarly, in literature and in the movies, there is a protagonist and an antagonist. It's like art imitating life and life imitating art. Everywhere we look, we can see people who are on our side and maybe find people who feel like our fiercest rivals. I believe the reason so many movies are made about "mean girls" and mean people is that, many times, people *are* mean. But we don't have to allow them to stop our progress or steal our strength. While it's true that the devil—and some people who act like the devil—may want to derail your destiny or keep you from fulfilling your God-given purpose, it doesn't mean you have to give them permission to do it.

I don't advocate looking for a fairy godmother, a pumpkin that turns into a carriage, or mice that lead the way. But just like in the movies, any influence—good or bad—can change your outlook on life and ultimately change your decisions concerning things, especially important "God things." I do believe, however, that we can make God our number one advisor, mentor, and friend and be keenly aware of what He is saying in His *"still small voice"* as He whispers His will to us (1 Kings 19:11–13).

As I mentioned above, I need to be careful who I associate with. I was working in my house one time, and it seemed a bit too quiet. So, I decided to turn on the television for some "background noise." Before long, I realized some crazy things were coming across the airwaves. Immediately, I changed the channel. I felt in my heart that I needed to be careful about allowing an influence into my home when I should have been diligent to keep it far from me. In my desire for "company," I brought in something that made me feel unsettled and sad. Immediately, I began to pray it off and out of my house.

In a powerful way, that experience reminded me of my need to be careful of the company I keep because *the company I keep is the company that's keeping me*. Whether it's a pet, a human being, a television program, social media, or some other influence, I have a responsibility to fill my soul and my spirit with things that are uplifting and pleasing to God. While I love to listen to ministry friends talk and to read uplifting posts on social media, I need to be discerning about the content of other posts. In 1 Corinthians 15:33, Paul writes, *"But don't be so naïve—there is another saying you know well—bad company corrupts good habits"* (VOICE, emphasis is in the original).

> ### THE COMPANY I KEEP IS THE COMPANY THAT'S KEEPING ME.

For me, and maybe for you too, it's easy to get distracted or get into situations that are not really in our best interest. Proverbs 4:20–22 says, *"My child, pay attention to what I say. Listen carefully to my words. Don't lose sight of them. Let them penetrate deep into your heart, for they bring life to those who find them, and healing to their whole body"* (NLT).

Proverbs 4:23 instructs you to *"guard your heart above all else, for it determines the course of your life"* (NLT). Many times, I see and hear things that don't lift me up on the inside. As the old saying goes, "That's why God gave us two ears—one for things to go in and one for them to go out." I don't believe I will ever be able to escape hearing and seeing certain things, but that doesn't mean I have to let them get into my soul (mind, will, and emotions) and spirit (inmost being). I need to make the effort to be accountable for "garbage in, garbage out."

Keep in mind that your dream, your vision, your word from God may be just that—yours. It's for *you*. Not everyone will go along with your hopes or encourage you in your dreams. So, pray and be careful who you share them with. Always remember that you are in good company if you are in the company of the Lord, and He delights to hear what's in your heart.

WHO IS CINDERELLA? AND IS THERE REALLY A HAPPILY EVER AFTER?

The fairy tale "Cinderella" tells the story of a lovely young girl who found herself in the middle of a horrible situation with seemingly no place to go. Her wicked stepmother and stepsisters forced her to do laborious chores, and when she had a rare moment to relax, she sat among the cinders by the fireplace in the family's home.

You probably know the rest of the story. A fairy godmother appeared to Cinderella and arrayed her in a beautiful ball gown and glass slippers. Off Cinderella went, transformed from a common laborer into a gorgeous young woman who caught the eye of a charming prince. The fairy godmother warned her not to stay out past midnight, or her carriage would turn into a pumpkin. As she raced to get home in time, she dropped one of her glass slippers. When the prince sought the owner of the slipper, it didn't fit anyone except Cinderella. She married the prince, and, of course, they lived happily ever after.

Not only is this fairy tale a story of Prince Charming, happily ever after, and great risk, it's a story about making a difficult decision. While the name "Cinder-Ella" was intended as a put-down to the young woman, no one could *keep* her down. Then, one day, Cinderella wore a gown, met a prince, danced until midnight, taught us the importance of shoes, and found her way to a happily ever after. She went from being mistreated and being called names to being the wife of a prince. And she taught us how to dream. But the dream came with a price, and the price was the decision to go to the ball. No one could make that decision for her. She had to decide for herself.

Hebrews 11:1 says, *"Faith is the substance of things hoped for, the evidence of things not seen."* Some people saw Cinderella as only a servant girl by the ashes. But Cinderella was more than what appeared before them. She was brave and kind and made hard choices. She went to the ball without a single guarantee of the life of happiness it would eventually lead to. Many of us, like Cinderella, are only seen as the sum total of our current circumstances, lacking the full vision of the amazing possibilities that lie before us. The unseen things in our lives are evident to God, and we were made for more than just sitting by the ashes. Just as Cinderella had to make her journey to the ball, it's up to us to start our own journey toward realizing our dreams.

Cinderella experienced self-doubt, and self-doubt can devastate dreams before they ever get started. There may be people who don't understand your dreams. When this happens, keep in mind that it's *your* dream, not theirs. Remember that Prince Charming was meant for Cinderella, no matter what other people thought about it or who doubted it.

Achieving your dreams, goals, and your happily ever after may or may not meet with the support of those around you. But if it's supported by God, you can go to the ball with confidence. As Romans 8:31 says, *"If God is for us, who can be against us?"* You and God can be a majority.

Cinderella was a dreamer, but she was not always surrounded by other dreamers or people who even supported her dreams in the slightest way. Yet, seemingly out of nowhere, unusual provision came to her. Now, in no way am I saying to look for a fairy godmother to support your dreams. But let's look at this from the perspective of a bigger support system. We don't need to look to a fairy godmother because we have a heavenly Father. We need to recognize who God is, what He has done for us, and how He loves us. We need to stir our faith in what we believe He is capable of doing. If a fairy-tale girl from the ashes can make so many people believe in dreams, how much more should we believe and demonstrate the power, goodness, and ability of our heavenly Father? And how much more should we demonstrate His power, goodness, and ability to the people in our world so they can believe also?

The choices you have made or the choices that were made for you don't have to be your final outcome. It's like my friend Tim Storey says: you can let your "setbacks become your comebacks." I believe you can join forces with God and His plan for your life, and rewrite your stories by having faith in Him and believing He can write a happily-ever-after ending that is perfect for you.

> I BELIEVE YOU CAN JOIN FORCES WITH GOD AND HIS PLAN FOR YOUR LIFE, AND REWRITE YOUR STORIES BY HAVING FAITH IN HIM.

FOR SUCH A TIME AS THIS

Part of our strength comes from realizing that God writes the stories and the endings in our lives. If we allow it, God can have the last word. He certainly got the final word in the story of Esther. But as with any good story, hers has tension and suspense. The outcome of her story came through the choices she was willing to make.

When we look at the story of Queen Esther and the journey it took for her to find her happily ever after, we see that wisdom, bravery, and obedience defined her success. While some people compare Queen Esther to Cinderella, their challenges and rewards on the journey to the throne were completely different. And just like Esther and Cinderella, the journey to your ultimate reward is most likely different from anyone else's.

Let's walk through Esther's story together. Esther was a beautiful young orphan whose name was Hadassah. She lived in

Persia under King Ahasuerus, who had the power to rule, reign, and make difficult decisions. King Ahasuerus was searching for a wife. Esther was not of royal birth. She wasn't even Persian, and she certainly was not in line to be queen. She was a most unlikely candidate for royalty, but through a series of unusual events, she was selected as one of many young women from among whom the king would eventually choose his new queen. And, eventually, he chose her.

Unfortunately, the king's closest advisor, Haman, hated people of Esther's heritage and worked diligently to destroy them. Esther's uncle, Mordecai, was of course distraught over this development, and he sent word to Esther, encouraging her to intervene—to appeal to the king to protect her people. He went so far as to say, "*Yet who knows whether you have come to the kingdom for such a time as this?*" (Esther 4:14). In other words, "Maybe asking the king to intervene with the situation at hand is the whole reason you are queen in the first place."

At that time, Esther knew that approaching the king without being summoned could end with an entirely different outcome than her "happily ever after." But this is a story of the bigger picture, the greater good. After fasting and praying for three days, along with Mordecai, her attendants, and others in the city, she decided to take a risk on behalf of her people.

To the casual observer, Esther may have looked like a Cinderella-type character—a poor girl who married a king to fulfill her own dream. But it's really the story of God placing her where He needed her to fulfill *His* purpose, and of her facing a fear that could have devastated her. Before her happily ever after could appear, her "for such a time as this" had to happen.

Fear is often the first giant to overcome before dreams can come true and destinies can be realized. Perhaps it is fear of failure or fear of finances or fear of some other inadequacy. Or even a simple question of "Why me, Lord?" In my experience, fear and doubt have an amazing way of showing up just before the ball. Esther must have wondered why God chose her. Why was she placed in that position? But in a moment of godly strength and encouragement, she rose to the challenge. She decided to answer God's call and go to the ball. Esther was beautiful, for sure. But she wasn't beautiful so she could be a queen. She was beautiful because she was born to save a nation. And her beauty was an important element in her journey. The rest of her story, as they say, is history. The king extended his golden scepter to her and called her forward. He spared her people, and the nation was saved.

If you are in a "for-such-a-time-as-this" decision-making situation, I encourage you to meditate on Proverbs 31:25, which says, *"She is clothed with strength and dignity, and she laughs without fear of the future"* (NLT).

SUMMARY

1. Be careful about the company you keep. It's important to have godly, positive, supportive people around you. Fill your soul and spirit with things that are uplifting and pleasing to God. *"But don't be so naïve—there's another saying you know well—bad company corrupts good habits"* (1 Corinthians 15:33 VOICE).

2. As in the story of Cinderella, achieving your dreams, goals, and your happily ever after may or may not meet with the support of those around you. But if you're supported by God, you can go to the ball with confidence. *"If God is for us, who can be against us?"* (Romans 8:31).

3. If we allow it, God can have the last word in the ending of our stories. But like Cinderella and Esther, you may have to overcome the giant called fear and choose to "go to the ball" and do what God has called you to do "*for such a time as this*" (Esther 4:14). As you choose to embrace your God-given destiny, have faith in God to produce your happily ever after.

NOTES TO SELF

Now that you've read this chapter, what notes would you like to write to yourself to help you remember the strength-building points that are most helpful to you or that apply to a specific situation in your life?

_____

_____

_____

_____

_____

YOU CAN FILL YOUR THOUGHT
LIFE, YOUR MENTAL REAL
ESTATE, WITH THE TRUTH
OF GOD'S WORD,
FAITH IN HIS GOODNESS, AND
THE KNOWLEDGE THAT
YOU CAN TRUST HIM IN
EVERY SITUATION.

5

STRONG WOMEN MAXIMIZE THEIR MENTAL REAL ESTATE

Most of all, let the Word of God fill you and renew your mind every day. When our minds are on Christ, Satan has little room to maneuver.
—Billy Graham[1]

In the children's book *The Little Engine That Could*, the engine said repeatedly, "I think I can. I think I can" until his task was complete. I read this book to my daughter Jordan so often that when she was learning to speak, she would say, "I sunk a tan. I sunk a tan." Her lips spoke these words incorrectly, but her heart and soul knew exactly what she was communicating. She was saying, "I think I can. I think I can."

When Jordan started school, one of her first spelling lessons included memorizing a list of words that began with the letter *b*. As she told me about this, she began to dance around the house, saying, "I can learn the 'b' word because I know the 'I' word." I did not understand, so I asked her what the "I" word had to do with learning the "b" words on the spelling list. She replied, "I can learn the 'b' words because 'I' can do all things through Christ who strengthens me." Lesson learned. To this day, Jordan has kept that same I-can-do-all-things, positive, happy attitude no matter the task at hand.

BRAIN SPACE

Throughout this chapter, when I write about mental real estate or brain space, I am talking about your thought life according to the Bible. As we move forward, I want you to consider how you are approaching your mental real estate by comparing it to God's Word and what He says you should think about the world, yourself, God, family, and so forth.

We all have a certain amount of "brain space"—our capacity to process or think about things. I call this our mental real estate. Our minds can only hold so many thoughts and ideas before they become crowded, and we become befuddled.

I believe that strong godly women learn how to discipline their minds and their thinking in ways that align with God's Word to benefit themselves and others. This is so important because a thought usually leads to an action, and actions can determine the outcomes of our situations.

MENTAL MONOPOLY

A portion of Proverbs 23:7 in the King James Version says, "*For as he thinketh in his heart, so is he.*" This verse has sometimes been used to communicate the importance of the way we think and manage our mental real estate. If we become what we think, perhaps this is a warning to carefully consider our thoughts and line them up with God's Word.

There are conflicting stories about the invention of the real estate board game Monopoly, with many stories attributing its creation to a man named Charles Darrow, who developed it not long after the crash of the stock market in 1929. Regardless of its origin, people have played and enjoyed Monopoly for generations. The point of the game is for players to attempt to increase their wealth and decrease their opponents' wealth (hopefully forcing them into bankruptcy) through purchasing and developing pieces of property, some of which are more valuable and profitable than others.

One lesson we can learn from Monopoly and the real estate market in general is the importance of location, location, location. Consider your thoughts or brain space as an empty game board that allows you to fill each location with whatever you choose. How valuable is your real estate? Do you have Monopoly mentality or constant clutter in the valuable space called your thoughts? Do you only fill your real estate with thoughts about the stress of your job, your past, or your problems? Is your thought life, your mental real estate, consumed with failures and missed opportunities? Do you think, "I'll never 'pass Go and collect $200'"?

Or are you willing to move forward? What is your mental Monopoly board, and how are you processing your mental real estate? If you are not progressing toward your goals, consider metaphorically packing your bags and moving forward to the next space ahead. You can do this by processing what you are thinking about through the filter of the Word of God. You can fill your thought life, your mental real estate, with the truth of God's Word, faith in His goodness, and the knowledge that you can trust Him in every situation.

If Charles Darrow could achieve his dreams in the middle of unemployment, the crash of the stock market, and the initial rejection of his heartfelt invention due to fifty-two fundamental errors, then you, like Darrow, can move past your obstacles and achieve your goals with the right mindset and God's help.[2]

EDEN, CANAAN, AND THE CROSS

There are three biblical places I want you to consider. I believe that when you understand their purpose, it can help you to see your potential become your reality and your prayer request become your praise report.

> SEE YOUR POTENTIAL BECOME YOUR REALITY AND YOUR PRAYER REQUEST BECOME YOUR PRAISE REPORT.

EDEN

The first location is the garden of Eden. When God created the earth, He put in it everything we could possibly need. It included every physical provision, from food and animals to family, and indeed every living thing. Once God created Adam, He placed him in the garden of Eden and created Eve as his wife. Although Adam worked, he never toiled, and all his needs were met. He faced no need that was not already provided for. God gave him the finest location, location, location.

As Adam and Eve grew spiritually and mentally and possessed Eden, they thrived. However, in time, they wanted more. Eve's thoughts were corrupted by lies from a snake, and she did the only thing God asked Adam and Eve *not* to do—eat from the Tree of Knowledge of Good and Evil. It was mankind's first step outside of God's will; it was sin—and it began with a thought. Unfortunately, because of their deliberate disobedience against God, Adam and Eve were forced to leave their paradise. But God, in His mercy, led their descendants to a new location for a second chance.

CANAAN

Fast-forward many years, and the second location is Canaan, a city whose builder and maker was the Lord (Hebrews 11:10). The Bible describes this magnificent dwelling place as *"a land flowing with milk and honey"* (Exodus 3:8). Canaan was so prosperous a land that two men were required to use a pole to transport even one cluster of grapes (Numbers 13:23).

To me, this illustration fits the idea in Ephesians 3:20 that God will do *"exceedingly abundantly"* far above anything we ask or think. Sadly, through disobedience, God's people lost this location, as well, and had to start over again.

When the Israelites reached the border of Canaan, they sent spies into the land to assess its inhabitants and defenses. However, after the report of the spies, the Israelites became afraid due to the presence of formidable opponents described as giants. As a result of their fear and lack of faith in God's promise to give them the land, they were forced to wander in the wilderness for forty years before entering Canaan. They listened to the wrong voices and made the wrong choices. They missed an opportunity for a blessing because they *thought* they knew better than God.

THE CROSS

In typical God fashion, He had the next location—the cross— already prepared. In order to create a place for believers to live abundantly on earth and then eternally in heaven, God sent His Son, Jesus, to secure and conquer the most important location in the world—the cross of Calvary.

Never before, and never since, has there ever been a sacrifice such as the one Jesus made on the cross. He did not make it to secure His future location, but to secure ours. Now, because of God's finest gift to us, we have a dwelling place that no person, no family problem, no economy, no politician, no work environment, and no situation can ever take away.

The apostle Paul, a New Testament writer, understood the importance of managing our thoughts. In Romans 12:2, he writes, *"And do not be conformed to this world, but be transformed by the renewing of your mind, so that you may prove what the will of God is, that which is good and acceptable and perfect"* (NASB). Jesus went to the cross to enable us to fulfill this Scripture in our lives.

The cross serves as a catalyst for transformation in our thinking. It isn't just a symbol; it's a game-changer. It speaks volumes about God's extravagant love and His commitment to us, and nothing else comes close. Standing in the shadow of the cross, our thoughts face a crossroads. We can choose to hold on to God's promises or get lost in the noise of the world. As the apostle Paul said, we have to renew our minds—and bring every thought under Christ's authority. In 2 Corinthians 10:4–5, he writes, "*The weapons we fight with are not the weapons of the world. On the contrary, they have divine power to demolish strongholds. We demolish arguments and every pretension that sets itself up against the knowledge of God, and we take captive every thought to make it obedient to Christ*" (NIV).

> THOSE WHO CLING TO THE MESSAGE OF THE CROSS FIND THEIR LIVES TRANSFORMED FROM THE INSIDE OUT. IT'S A FREEDOM THAT NOTHING ELSE CAN MATCH.

It's not just about what we think; it's about what we do with those thoughts. At the foot of the cross, our thoughts meet their possibilities head-on. Those who cling to the message of the cross find their lives transformed from the inside out. It's a freedom that nothing else can match.

In the Old Testament, Isaiah 26:3 says, in reference to God, "*You will keep in perfect peace those whose minds are steadfast, because they trust in you*" (NIV). God has given us the opportunity to be consistently focused on Him. The opportunity for perfect peace includes a qualifier, meaning we have to do something to receive the promise. We have to agree with what God says to reap the benefits of it. To live in God's perfect peace, we have to follow God's Word, get into godly obedience, and protect our thought life, as though our peace depends on it. Because, I believe, it does.

CONTROLLING OUR THOUGHT LIFE

I was once confronted by a disagreeable person who did not believe the message of Jesus. To say he was not a believer is an understatement. He wanted me to argue about Scriptures in the Bible and what they have to do with reality. He commented that Christianity is mind control. I replied, "You are exactly right. God gave me a wonderful opportunity to obey the Bible and take control of my mind, my will, and my emotions" (my soul). I told him I would highly recommend trying this because, to me, it's one of the greatest gifts God has ever given humanity. We have an opportunity to choose. And I want to choose perfect peace by keeping my mind stayed on my Father God and His Word.

In 2 Timothy 1:7, Paul writes, *"For God has not given us a spirit of fear, but of power and of love and of a sound mind."* In the *Amplified Bible, Classic Edition,* this verse reads, *"For God did not give us a spirit of timidity (of cowardice, of craven and cringing and fawning fear), but [He has given us a spirit] of power and of love and of calm and well-balanced mind and discipline and self-control."* One reason I love this Scripture so much is because it clearly shows that we have the power to choose what occupies our thought life.

Consider these Scriptures:

+ *"For as he thinketh in his heart, so is he"* (Proverbs 23:7 KJV).

+ *"Be anxious for nothing, but in everything by prayer and supplication, with thanksgiving, let your requests be made known to God; and the peace of God, which surpasses all understanding, will guard your hearts and minds through Christ Jesus"* (Philippians 4:6–7).

+ *"Finally, brethren, whatever things are true, whatever things are noble, whatever things are just, whatever things are pure, whatever things are lovely, whatever things are of good report, if there is any virtue and if there is anything praiseworthy—meditate on these things"* (Philippians 4:8).

+ *"The weapons we fight with are not the weapons of the world. On the contrary, they have divine power to demolish strongholds. We demolish arguments and every pretention that sets itself up against the knowledge of God, and we take captive every thought to make it obedient to Christ"* (2 Corinthians 10:4–5 NIV).

As we fill our thought life with God's Word, we can take captive ungodly thoughts to make them obedient to Christ.

AMAZING OPPORTUNITIES

We are often given amazing opportunities to choose between right and wrong, and the important thing is that we are given the opportunity to choose. Remember, in Joshua 24:15, Joshua says to the Israelites, *"Choose for yourselves this day whom you will serve.... But as for me and my house, we will serve the LORD."* We always have opportunities to serve God. The good news is the choice is ours.

I often make convenient, good, or bad choices based on human emotions. But I have found that my human decisions are not always God's highest and best for me. Sometimes I think my opinion and God's are on the same wavelength—and sometimes they are not. I often find that people, including myself, settle for less than God's best. The easy decision is not always God's decision.

Satan has a way of disguising his plans for our lives so strategically that we don't even know we've been duped. Yet, when we realize who we are in Christ, we can filter our decisions through the Word of God by the power of the Holy Spirit. The Spirit of God in us can lead us to make the decisions that are best for us.

I have found that one important lesson I had to learn is to listen to the *"still small voice"* of God (1 Kings 19:12) and not to the counterfeit thoughts the devil tries to deceive you with—no matter how appealing he tries to make them.

Let's close this chapter with Proverbs 3:5–6: *"Trust in the LORD with all your heart, and lean not on your own understanding; in all your ways acknowledge Him, and He shall direct your paths."* In *The Message* version of the Bible, this passage says, *"Trust GOD from the bottom of your heart; don't try to figure out everything on your own. Listen for GOD's voice in everything you do, everywhere you go; he's the one who will keep you on track."*

My prayer is that this chapter has encouraged you to evaluate your thought life, your mental real estate. Think of each thought as a square of property on the game board of your life. As you take inventory, ask yourself what occupies the valuable spaces in your thoughts. Make a list of the properties in your mind that are nonproductive or out of alignment with God's Word. Ask Him how to rethink or reprioritize those places and put into them what He would choose for you. Ask Him about location, location, location—what space should get your attention? Pray that He will show you where to apply your time, your talent, your efforts, and your finances. Which location would produce the highest rate of return for you and for His kingdom? Remember, our thoughts can lead to actions, and we want each thought to lead to an action that glorifies God.

Isaiah 55:9 says that God's thoughts and ways are higher than ours. Let's invite Him into our mental real estate and choose thoughts that align with His. When God does the thinking and the strategizing, I don't believe we have to "pass Go" or "collect $200." Instead, we get God's highest and best in everything He has for us. And when we have that, we can discover and live in our *true* strength.

SUMMARY

1. Think of your thoughts as an empty game board that allows you to fill each location with whatever you choose. If you are not progressing toward your God-given goals, consider changing the way you think. I encourage you to fill your mind with the truth of God's Word, faith in His goodness, and the knowledge that you can trust Him in every situation.

2. To get to the place where you have a calm, disciplined, controlled, well-balanced mind, give the devil no place (Ephesians 4:27). Fill your mind with the Word of God and take ungodly thoughts captive to make them obedient to Christ (2 Corinthians 10:5).

3. Isaiah 55:9 says God's thoughts and ways are higher than ours. Consider inviting Him into your thought life and choosing thoughts that align with His. When God does the thinking and the strategizing, you get God's highest and best. And when you have that, you can discover and live in your *true* strength.

NOTES TO SELF

Now that you've read this chapter, what notes would you like to write to yourself to help you remember the strength-building points that are most helpful to you or that apply to a specific situation in your life?

_____

_____

_____

_____

_____

IF YOU WILL DEVELOP THE
HABIT OF STUDYING THE LIFE
AND MINISTRY OF JESUS, YOU
WILL SEE HIM RISING UP OUT
OF THE PAGES OF THE BIBLE
IN NEW AND EXCITING WAYS.

6

STRONG WOMEN BELIEVE IN MIRACLES

Expect a miracle. Expect a new miracle every day.
—Oral Roberts

The best lesson I ever learned about prayer came from my father-in-law, Oral Roberts. He grew up in a poverty-stricken area of Oklahoma. He explained his family's economic status by referencing their extreme poverty. He spent much of his youth picking cotton, and, occasionally, he showed me the scars on his arms, scars inflicted by the sharp bracts on the cotton plants. He said the scars always reminded him that there had to be a way out of poverty.

At age seventeen, Oral was stricken with tuberculosis, a deadly, contagious disease. He was convinced that he would never get out of poverty and wouldn't even live to see his eighteenth birthday. His body had shriveled to 117 pounds on a frame well over six feet tall. In his day, the medicines we now have to treat tuberculosis were not available, so his family made the difficult decision to take him to a tuberculosis sanitarium to die. The paperwork had already been signed when his older brother Elmer heard of a "healing evangelist" holding a "tent revival" in nearby Ada, Oklahoma. Miracles were happening in these meetings. People were being healed.

Arrangements were made to get Oral to the tent revival at any cost. And for the Roberts family, the cost was high. Just before Oral left home, his sister Jewel went into his room to deliver seven simple words: "Oral, God is going to heal you."

To which he replied, "Is He, Jewel?"

And Jewel, confident in faith, said, "Yes!"

Jewel's faith-filled words set something on fire in the soul of the dying teenager, and the trip was on. Elmer borrowed a car and put in thirty-five cents' worth of gas. He wrapped his youngest brother in a mattress, as Oral was too weak to sit up, put him in the back seat, and made the drive to Ada.

"LOOSE HIM AND LET HIM GO FREE"

Oral said he was so sick he barely understood the sermon that night. But he never forgot the prayer that was prayed for him. With full power and authority, the evangelist said, "You foul, tormenting disease, come out of this boy's body. Loose him and let him go free." Oral had never heard a prayer like that before, nor did he have any idea it could be prayed over *his* dying body.

Oral was healed that night. The blood in his lungs dried up, and the coughing stopped. A divine intervention, a miracle from God, took place. And the rest, as they say, is history.

IT CAN HAPPEN TO YOU

Oral made many simple observations and statements that affected people in powerful ways. I heard them before I ever met him, and they made a profound difference in my life. One of them was, "Something good is going to happen to you," and another was,

"Expect a miracle." I'd like you to personalize these statements by saying, "Something good is going to happen to me," and "I expect a miracle in my life." Acts 10:34 says that *"God is no respecter of persons"* (KJV), meaning that He does not show partiality. He can do miracles for anyone who believes and trusts Him. I believe you are just as much a candidate for a miracle as anyone else.

I hope you will take this invitation seriously and begin to say that you believe something good will happen to you and that you expect a miracle in your life. There's no magic formula for doing it. There is, however, a biblical one found in Romans 10:17, which states, *"Faith comes from hearing the message, and the message is heard through the word about Christ"* (NIV). You simply have to believe that God is who He says He is and expect it for yourself. This may be a new way of thinking for you, so as God leads you to make these positive declarations, simply speak them out loud. My hope is that the more you speak them, the more you will believe them.

In addition, I believe that if you will develop the habit of studying the life and ministry of Jesus, you will see Him rising up out of the pages of the Bible in new and exciting ways. You will increasingly realize who He is and how much He loves you. I pray that you will truly find your identity in Christ when you discover who He is in you.

GOD IS THE WORKER OF MIRACLES

Oral Roberts's encouragement to expect a miracle was so simple yet so profound. Later, he added to this phrase, "Expect a *new* miracle every day!" I regard a miracle as a divine intervention that can't be overlooked or explained.

Expecting a miracle may seem impossible to you. A miracle may be the furthest thing from your mind. But I'd like it to be the closest. I believe that if we work at it, we can change the way we think. We can begin to think that miracles are possible and to live every day of our lives with a miracle mentality—a godly determination to *expect* a miracle.

In our ministry, over the last couple of decades, we've received so many miracle testimonies that they are almost difficult to count. Many of the miraculous things God has done in people's lives can be attributed to miracle thinking.

I want you to discover that your true strength comes from God, and God is the worker of miracles. When we rely on God, acknowledging Him as the source of the answers, the breakthroughs, and the miracles we need in our lives—well, it's kind of like Popeye and the can of spinach. We can realize that we are stronger than we think and that, as believers, we belong to the One who works miracles and makes all things possible (Matthew 19:26).

"THE BEGGAR OF JOS" HEALED

On a trip to Nigeria, I witnessed what I consider to be the greatest miracle I've ever seen. Richard had been preaching to a large crowd in the city of Jos, and we were receiving testimonies of one miracle after another. People came onto the platform to testify about what had happened to them. Suddenly, the crowd erupted with spontaneous cheering. Richard and I had no idea what was happening when a young man came onto the platform and began to jump up and down, then crouch down, jump up and down, then crouch down.

Our interpreter went to talk to the young man, and we learned that his name was Abdul. The townspeople knew him as "the Beggar of Jos." He had been unable to walk since birth, and his parents had carried him to the post office daily to beg for money. But at the service that night, there he was, jumping up and down before a large crowd who knew he was unable to walk.

Richard and I ended up jumping and praising God as Abdul testified that he was healed and could walk. The next day, the newspaper carried the story with a headline that read, "Beggar of Jos Healed."

This reminds me of the story in John 5:5–9 when Jesus healed the man who was unable to walk. The same Jesus who healed the man in that story and the Beggar of Jos is the same Jesus still healing today (Hebrews 13:8).

NO SITTING DUCKS HERE. EXPECT A MIRACLE!

A couple of years ago, I was unpacking boxes when I noticed I had a lump in my throat. Several people in the building where I worked had strep throat, so I wondered if I had it too. It had been years since I had strep throat, but I thought, "Well, it's possible, so I'd better get a strep test."

I called my doctor, had a strep test, and thought nothing of it. The test results came back negative. But by that time, an unusual gray hue had begun to come over my skin. It was hard to explain, but I looked as though I had no natural coloring—just an odd gray color.

On my doctor's advice, I called a friend in the medical field and agreed to undergo more tests. Examinations and symptoms pointed to the fact that my thyroid wasn't behaving properly. I needed additional testing, including an ultrasound and a lot of other things.

During that time, I went to my daughter's house one day and began to climb a flight of stairs. I had to stop halfway up. My energy level was zero. Almost immediately after that, my phone rang, and I was not prepared for what would happen in the next few minutes. Before I knew it, the lady on the phone told me that I had thyroid cancer and needed to have my thyroid removed immediately.

Other tests indicated additional health issues, and I soon found myself in a juggling act trying to decide along with the doctors which situation needed to be addressed first for the best outcome.

I wasn't prepared to hear that I had thyroid cancer. I do remember my knees buckling under me, and my family looking at me, wondering what was wrong. As soon as I could get my thoughts together, I explained to them what was going on. While everything inside of me felt defeated, frightened, and overwhelmed by a host of other emotions that I didn't know were hiding inside of me, my family literally rushed to me and started to pray. They began to speak life over me, decree that they would not accept anything but a positive outcome, and declare that God would take care of me.

The impact of their words of hope and encouragement cannot be explained in human terms. What that meant to me cut through my thoughts and fears and went straight into my soul, and even deeper into my spirit.

Soon after the diagnosis, Richard went to a toy store and bought me a little yellow rubber duck. He gave it to me and said, "You are not a sitting duck. You are the righteousness of God in Christ Jesus. Now, Lindsay, expect a miracle." He went on to remind me that whatever I needed, God was able to provide. From that moment on, I had a mindset for miracles.

A friend of mine in Texas is a cancer survivor and a woman of God who has helped many people deal with cancer and find solutions. She walked me through everything she went through when she was diagnosed, and she understood what I was dealing with. But our conversation wasn't focused primarily on cancer; it was ultimately centered on miracles.

Today, I am healthy and so grateful to my family for never giving up hope and not allowing me to stay in fear. And I'm so grateful to God for His miracle-working power.

BEGIN TO SAY THAT YOU
BELIEVE SOMETHING GOOD
WILL HAPPEN TO YOU AND
THAT YOU EXPECT A MIRACLE
IN YOUR LIFE.

In my case, this particular miracle came in the form of being declared cancer free. However, I've seen God's miracle power working in so many other ways as well. I've seen financial miracles, physical miracles, emotional miracles, spiritual miracles, and miracles that I can't even begin to explain.

HEALING FOR EVERY AREA OF YOUR LIFE

Let's think about rain for a moment. When rain falls, it waters everything in its path. I believe healing is the same way. When people think about healing, they often think about physical healing. Physical healing is wonderful, but, again, healing can be spiritual, financial, emotional, relational, or in any other area of our lives.

Psalm 138:8 says, "*The Lord will perfect that which concerns me.*" And 1 John 3:8 says, "*For this purpose the Son of God was manifested, that He might destroy the works of the devil.*" I believe these verses give us great hope for healing and miracles in our lives.

Visualize a train with four sets of wheels on the track. If three sets of wheels are running perfectly, but the fourth slips off the track, the train can be headed for a disaster. Similarly, if most of the areas of our life are fabulous, but one situation is "off the track," we can have a problem. I believe that God wants to fix those areas so our life becomes a smooth ride. Therefore, my prayer for you is that "*the God of peace Himself* [will] *sanctify you through and through*" (1 Thessalonians 5:23 AMPC).

Psalm 107:20 says, "*He sent his word and healed them, and delivered them from their destructions.*" The *Oxford Pocket Dictionary of Current English* defines *destruction* as "the action or process of causing so much damage to something that it no longer exists or cannot be repaired."[1] Wow. The dictionary describes *destruction* as "irreparable," yet God delivers us from our destructions. Regarding whatever damage and evil that tries to come against us,

God's Word says He has chosen to heal us for His glory and for our good. I believe when we recognize that God wants miracles, signs, and wonders to be part of our everyday lives, that's when they can be.

> WHEN WE RECOGNIZE THAT WE CAN STOP FOCUSING ON OUR PROBLEMS AND SWITCH TO THE SOLUTIONS, I BELIEVE THAT'S WHEN JESUS CAN DO WHAT HE DOES BEST—MIRACLES, SIGNS, AND WONDERS.

I like to say that what we focus on will develop—will manifest in our lives. When we focus on fear, worry, destruction, problems, and more problems, we can give these things the wrong amount of emphasis in our lives. But when we recognize that we can stop focusing on our problems and switch to the solutions, I believe that's when Jesus can do what He does best—miracles, signs, and wonders.

Throughout our lifetime, we have opportunities to believe. We can believe in each other; we can believe in Santa Claus; we can believe in the Easter Bunny; we can believe in the power of prayer; we can believe in miracles. What we focus on can become so much a part of what we believe. I encourage you to focus on Psalm 107:20 today and believe that God is capable of sending His Word to heal us everywhere we hurt and to deliver us from any destruction the devil sends our way. Ephesians 3:20 teaches us that God is capable of doing *"exceedingly abundantly"* far above anything we dare ask or think. I'd like to ask for and think about miracles. There is more than enough time and there are more than enough reasons to focus on our problems. But I choose to focus on the miracles. Perhaps that's why I've seen so many miracles in my lifetime and why I want so much for you to see miracles in yours.

SUMMARY

1. Start saying aloud, "Something good is going to happen to me" and "I expect a miracle in my life." According to Acts 10:34, God doesn't show partiality. He can do miracles for anyone who believes and trusts Him. He can do miracles for you.

2. I believe we can change the way we think. We can think miracles are possible and live every day with a miracle mentality—a godly determination to *expect* a miracle. I pray you will discover that your true strength comes from God, and God is the worker of miracles.

3. Are you feeling discouraged? I encourage you to rely on God, acknowledging Him as the source of the answers, the breakthroughs, and the miracles you need in your life. I pray you will realize that you are stronger than you think and that you belong to the One who works miracles and makes all things possible (Matthew 19:26).

4. A miracle is a divine intervention that can't be overlooked or explained. Psalm 107:20 says, *"He sent his word and healed them, and delivered them from their destructions."* I want you to realize that the Bible says it is God's will to heal you.

NOTES TO SELF

Now that you've read this chapter, what notes would you like to write to yourself to help you remember the strength-building points that are most helpful to you or that apply to a specific situation in your life?

_____

_____

_____

_____

_____

USING WISDOM IN WHAT WE
SAY CAN KEEP US SAFE AND
HELP US MAKE OUR WAY TO
WHERE GOD WANTS TO TAKE
US IN OUR LIVES.

7

STRONG WOMEN USE THEIR WORDS WISELY

Change your language, change your life.
—Lindsay Roberts

My daughter Jordan was so young she could hardly speak, but her spirit had heard Richard and me talk about the importance and power of words. Before she could make a sentence, she would simply say, "Word-a-word, word-a-word." As silly as her cute little babbling sounded, I believe she was practicing the value of her words.

Proverbs 31 is often referred to as the biblical description of a godly woman. Verse 26 of this chapter describes a godly woman this way: *"She opens her mouth with wisdom, and on her tongue is the law of kindness."* Strong godly women use their words wisely, and that's what I encourage you to do. I love the word *encourage*, and I hope you take it to heart, because I didn't choose it haphazardly. I chose it to spark something in you, and that something is encouragement. I pray that the "word lessons" you read in this chapter will leave a giant impact on your word choices so that you begin to choose your words wisely, on purpose, and for a purpose—God's purpose.

WORDS MATTER

Let's face it: some people just love to talk. They try to engage anyone near them in conversation. They offer unsolicited advice and opinions. They want to keep talking in meetings, long after the business has been discussed. They chitchat at sporting events, church services, or in line at the grocery store. They may not think much about what they say; they just want to say something.

In Matthew 12:36, Jesus refers to the words of such people as *"idle"* (NKJV), *"empty"* (NIV), or *"careless"* (ESV). We may think words we speak casually are small and unimportant, but I believe the words we speak *are* important. Jesus says in the Scripture I referred to above: *"But I tell you that everyone will have to give account on the day of judgment for every empty word they have spoken. For by your words you will be acquitted, and by your words you will be condemned"* (Matthew 12:36–37 NIV). King Solomon, known as the wisest man who ever lived, writes in Song of Solomon 2:15 that it's *"the little foxes"* that destroy the vines. In other words, little things can be extremely important.

I've heard that people in general may speak approximately sixteen thousand words per day. It's easy to think, "That's a lot of words to be held accountable for," and it is! If we're going to speak sixteen thousand words a day, we have sixteen thousand opportunities to speak something that is wise and edifying to others instead of something foolish and destructive. We have sixteen thousand opportunities to declare the Word of God in every situation in which we find ourselves.

AVIATION JARGON

In 1956, the International Civil Aviation Organization (ICAO) created a language for the aviation world to adhere to so they could communicate with one another universally.[1] This aviation language was developed to alleviate any misinterpretation of flight commands. The language is so specific, it even includes its own alphabet (such as "Alfa" for *A*, "Bravo" for *B*, "Charlie" for *C*, and others) as well as a communication system specifically and universally in English. With many lives at stake every time a plane takes flight, proper communication is vital.

Aviation personnel know never to deviate from the words that are part of their language. They are required to use their agreed-upon jargon in order to fly successfully and avoid disaster. Their agreement to use specific words is so important that, without it, they cannot operate an aircraft. If airplane pilots understand the importance and value of their words enough to have a set of rules that govern how they use them, how much more should we as Christians understand the value of our words and be careful about the way we use them?

As a believer, I can speak a language that may seem foreign to the world around me. It's the language we read in God's Word, the language of faith. When I entered into a personal relationship with God, everything inside of my world changed. Many of those changes manifested in external ways—in my decisions, in my priorities, in the way I treated other people, and certainly in my speech. As I learned the Word of God and gleaned from His wisdom, I began measuring my circumstances by His Word rather than by reflecting on the ways of the world. When my words changed, my focus followed.

Just as aviation jargon keeps pilots, crews, and passengers safe so they can get to the places they need to go, using wisdom in what we say can keep us safe and help us make our way to where God wants to take us in our lives.

> GOD DESIGNED HIS WORD TO WORK, TO
> SUCCEED AND FULFILL ITS PURPOSE.

WORDS ARE POWERFUL

Over the years, I have realized how important it is for my words to line up with God's Word. Jeremiah 1:12 says that God is *"watching over"* His word *"to perform it"* (ESV). Isaiah 55:10–11 says:

> For as the rain comes down, and the snow from heaven, and do not return there, but water the earth, and make it bring forth and bud, that it may give seed to the sower and bread to the eater, so shall My word be that goes forth from My mouth; it shall not return to Me void, but it shall accomplish what I please, and it shall prosper in the thing for which I sent it.

This tells me that God designed His Word to work, to succeed and fulfill its purpose. And if I want the success of His Word in my life, I must make sure my words line up with His words— that what I say about myself, other people, my life, my future, the world, and everything else agrees with what He says.

As we consider the words we speak, Psalm 19:14 offers us a wonderful prayer to pray each day: *"Let the words of my mouth and the meditation of my heart be acceptable in Your sight, O LORD, my strength and my Redeemer."*

THE LEMON THEORY

Proverbs 6:2 says we are *"snared,"* or trapped, by our words. While someone may read this and think it's a bad thing, I see it as a great thing. Whenever we receive instruction from God's Word about what to do or not do, it's valuable. The better we understand that our words can ensnare us, the more carefully we can choose them.

I like to think about this in terms of what I call the "lemon theory." Let me explain it by asking a couple of questions: First, what do you get when you squeeze a lemon? You get whatever is inside of it. Just like that lemon, what do we get when we are squeezed—when we are under stress? We get whatever is inside of us. Whatever we are full of comes out of us—perhaps in thoughts or feelings, in facial expressions or gestures, in behaviors, and certainly in words. The words that circulate on the inside of us make their way to the external world.

My daughter Jordan is a worship leader with a beautiful voice. When people listen to her sing, they say it brings peace to the atmosphere. The interesting thing is that if you knew Jordan as a person, you would refer to her personality as a peacemaker. It's no wonder that the peace of God comes out in her music. According to the "lemon theory," because Jordan fills her life with the peace of God, it comes pouring out when she sings. I want to encourage you to recognize what is on the inside of you so that you can develop it as a strength on the outside.

That is why I believe these three Scriptures are so vital to our well-being:

1. *"Your word I have **hidden in my heart**, that I might not sin against You"* (Psalm 119:11).

2. *"A good person produces good things from the treasury of a good heart, and an evil person produces evil things from the treasury of an evil heart. What you say flows from what is in your heart"* (Luke 6:45 NLT).

3. *"The tongue can bring death or life; those who love to talk will reap the consequences"* (Proverbs 18:21 NLT).

To me, hiding God's Word in my heart means reading it, studying it, memorizing it, and obeying it. I believe Solomon understood this because he wrote in Proverbs 4:23, *"Above all else, guard your heart, for everything you do flows from it"* (NIV). If we've hidden God's Word in our hearts, everything we do and say should flow from it, building a treasury of godly principles and good things. Then we can speak life and enjoy the results of our

Bible-based, life-giving words—not only when we feel metaphorically squeezed or under pressure but in every situation.

GOD'S WORD GIVES WISDOM

The first place I turn to when I need wisdom for any reason in any circumstance is God's Word. From Genesis to Revelation, there's wisdom to be gained from this Book. The book of Proverbs is considered one of the Bible's "Wisdom books," along with Job, Psalms, Ecclesiastes, and Song of Solomon. Ecclesiastes, Song of Solomon, and much of Proverbs are believed to have been written by Solomon, who, as I noted earlier, is viewed as the wisest person who ever lived. If this is true, wouldn't it be prudent and productive for us to follow his advice?

In Proverbs 4:20–22, Solomon writes: *"My son, give attention to my words; incline your ear to my sayings. Do not let them depart from your eyes; keep them in the midst of your heart; for they are life to those who find them, and health to all their flesh."* These verses tell us to give attention to God's Word, which is great. But they are specific as to why we should pay so much attention to the words of wisdom: because *"they are* **life** *to those who find them, and* **health** *to all their flesh"* (Proverbs 4:22).

> **STRONG GODLY WOMEN CHOOSE THEIR WORDS** *ON* **PURPOSE AND** *FOR* **GOD'S PURPOSES.**

In the *New International Version*, Proverbs 4 begins with the heading, "Get Wisdom at Any Cost." I believe this is great advice. When we get wisdom, we speak wisely. Take a look at some of what Proverbs says about foolish words:

Fools vent their anger, but the wise quietly hold it back.

(Proverbs 29:11 NLT)

Fools find no pleasure in understanding but delight in airing their own opinions. (Proverbs 18:2 NIV)

Even fools are thought wise if they keep silent, and discerning if they hold their tongues. (Proverbs 17:28 NIV)

The tongue of the wise uses knowledge rightly, but the mouth of fools pours forth foolishness. (Proverbs 15:2)

Strong godly women choose their words *on* purpose and *for* God's purposes.

GOD'S WISDOM GIVES US STRENGTH

When my daughter Chloe was about nine years old, she finally made it into the "big time" in terms of horseback riding. She'd worked hard, and, for the first time ever, she could put a saddle on the horse and ride in circles in the arena. One day, she entered a show with several other competitors, and they all had the same plan: ride in circles and hope to win a ribbon.

Chloe was riding an Arabian horse that had seen many years in show jumping competitions and had been, as they say, put out to pasture. This horse had been retired from bigger competitions perhaps longer than Chloe had been alive. His name was Wisdom, which we found quite unique.

The great thing about Wisdom was that he was too old to do anything dangerous, yet experienced enough to know how to walk in circles. But, somehow, the moment Wisdom got into the arena, he began to fulfill Psalm 103:5 in that his youth was *"renewed like the eagle's."* Wisdom began trotting around the arena like the proverbial spring chicken, like a colt looking for his mama. Chloe got out of step and was disqualified. As happens under such circumstances, the announcer excused her and asked her to leave the arena.

So, there was Chloe, with number 142 pinned to her shirt, exiting the arena in absolute defeat. The look on her face said it all. Richard and I took off as fast as we could go to console her, see if she was okay, and try to make sure this situation would not be devastating to her little wounded soul. When we got to her, we saw that she had jumped off the horse, walked in front of him while holding the reins, and put her hands on his jaw. Face-to-face with him, she said, "Wisdom, don't you *ever* embarrass me like that again!" Her words had such authority that Wisdom simply looked at her as if to say, "Yes, ma'am." And from that moment on, Chloe and Wisdom got along just fine.

Chloe's horse Wisdom demonstrated what the so-called wisdom of the world can do. It often leaves us defeated and maybe even embarrassed. But the wisdom of God is designed to lead us to success and blessing. Ecclesiastes 7:19 says, *"Wisdom makes one wise person more powerful than ten rulers in a city"* (NIV).

When we think, believe, act, and speak wisely, we can then reap the benefits of wisdom.

SUMMARY

1. Strong godly women use their words wisely. According to Matthew 12:36–37, the Lord will hold us accountable for our words. I encourage you to line up your words with what God says in His Word. Keep yourself on track by praying Psalm 19:14 each day: *"Let the words of my mouth and the meditation of my heart be acceptable in Your sight, O LORD, my strength and my Redeemer."*

2. What happens when you're "squeezed" by difficult situations? According to what I call the "lemon theory," when you speak, whatever you are full of will likely come pouring out of you. The best way I know to avoid having something ungodly emerge is to hide God's Word in your heart (Psalm 119:11): read it, study it, memorize it, and obey it.

3. Strong godly women avoid unwise speech. Use your words wisely, choosing them *on* purpose and *for* God's purposes. The Bible tells you, *"Get wisdom!"* (Proverbs 4:5), and the best place to find God's wisdom is in God's Word, especially in the Wisdom books believed to have been written by the wisest man of all, Solomon.

NOTES TO SELF

Now that you've read this chapter, what notes would you like to write to yourself to help you remember the strength-building points that are most helpful to you or that apply to a specific situation in your life?

_____

_____

_____

_____

_____

WHEN YOU NEED TO KNOW
WHAT TO SAY AND WHEN
TO SAY IT—OR NOT—I
ENCOURAGE YOU TO PRAY,
GET QUIET BEFORE THE
LORD, AND LISTEN FOR HIS
STILL SMALL VOICE BEARING
WITNESS WITH YOUR SPIRIT.

8

STRONG WOMEN SAY YES, NO, OR NOTHING AT ALL

*To everything there is a season, a time for every purpose
under heaven:... a time to keep silence, and a time to speak.*
—Ecclesiastes 3:1, 7

You and I have many choices to make regarding our communication each day. When we need to respond to a certain situation or question, or in the context of a conversation, we can say yes, we can say no, or we can say nothing at all. Sometimes our responses have little impact on our lives, such as, "No, I don't want to watch television tonight," and sometimes they change the trajectory of our future, such as, "Yes, I'll take the job in a foreign country." And sometimes, the wisest course of action is to say nothing at all, such as when you are in a situation that concerns you deeply, but you know that for some reason, your opinion wouldn't be well received, or when you pray about a response and feel God is leading you to speak to Him about it in prayer while not saying anything to the other people involved.

In many circumstances, it takes strength to say yes and strength to say no as God leads us. It also takes strength to say nothing at all when that's what He asks. As we discover our *true* strength in Him, responding appropriately can become easier. As we watch what happens as a result of our responses, we can grow in our reliance on God and in confidence that He leads us in every situation.

> *YES* IS POWERFUL. I THINK IT SHOULD COME
> WITH A ROLL OF CAUTION TAPE ATTACHED TO
> IT AND NOT BE USED LIGHTLY OR FRIVOLOUSLY.

SOMETIMES STRONG WOMEN SAY YES

There are times when the course of a woman's life depends on saying yes—even when it doesn't make sense to her (but she knows God is leading), and even when other people aren't supportive or don't understand.

At times, the world makes a big deal out of the word *yes*. For example, most people know what is meant when they hear, "She said yes!" or "Yes to the dress!"

Yes is powerful. I think it should come with a roll of caution tape attached to it and not be used lightly or frivolously.

YES TO AFRICA

After giving birth to my son and burying him thirty-six hours later, I had to decide what my next step would be. Richard had committed to go to Nigeria for a very large healing crusade, and I had planned to stay home with the baby. After our son died, I encouraged Richard to go while I stayed home to recover.

I was given an airline ticket to California and a place to stay where I could rest and recuperate in the sun. But as I was planning the trip to California, I felt the strongest urgency to join Richard in Nigeria. However, since I did not have the proper immunizations,

I would need to stay behind, get the required shots, and join him a week later.

The trip would include a stop in Senegal and another stop in the Ivory Coast. Since Richard would be going ahead of me, I would be traveling alone. At the last minute, a lady pastor from Africa decided to go on the same trip, so, technically, there would be someone else traveling with me. But I still felt very alone. Every imaginable thought for my situation whirled in my head. However, I could not get past the direction of the Holy Spirit. I talked it over with family members, and they thought I was crazy.

Then Richard and I went to Oral and asked for prayer. To my surprise, Oral believed that I was supposed to go. So, in a matter of days after giving birth, I boarded a plane to Africa. To the natural way of thinking, this seemed ridiculous. But I knew in my spirit that making the trip would put me in the right place at the right time. To this day, I can't tell you how I knew that or why I believed it to be true. I just knew I was supposed to say yes.

When I arrived in Nigeria, I was unexpectedly held at security in the airport. While my thoughts were swirling, my spirit was at peace. Richard was in Swaziland, so our dear friend Archbishop Benson Idahosa met me at the airport in Lagos, got me released from security, and took me to his home to stay with his wife, Dr. Margaret Idahosa.

The next day, Richard joined us, and we spent several days ministering in churches and praying for the large crowds that had gathered in the stadium. We saw miracle after miracle, including what I believe was the most phenomenal miracle I had ever witnessed when a young man who had been unable to walk since birth was miraculously healed. The remarkable thing was that as we prayed for people to be healed, my soul was being healed too.

YES TO NEW LIFE

After two miscarriages, multiple surgeries, and the death of our son, you can imagine I did not ever want to get pregnant or go through the devastation of losing a child again. However, after much prayer, Dr. Margaret encouraged me to try one more time and see the glory of God bring restoration to my situation. I agreed. Three beautiful daughters later, saying yes was one of the most important decisions I have ever made.

SOMETIMES STRONG WOMEN SAY NO

In a people-pleasing society, sometimes the word *no* can be perceived as an expression of stubbornness or rebellion. When people want to control a situation and someone says no to them, they might try to make that individual feel guilty for saying no when, in fact, no was the best answer for that person to give.

Not everybody will be thrilled when you stand up for yourself and say no when the Lord, common sense, or circumstances require you to do so. The word *yes* even sounds smoother and more pleasant than the word *no*. But *no* is not just a word recited by adorable two-year-olds. *No* can also be a strength-giving word when it is the proper, God-directed response.

> *NO* CAN ALSO BE A STRENGTH-GIVING
> WORD WHEN IT IS THE PROPER,
> GOD-DIRECTED RESPONSE.

INQUIRING OF THE LORD

When I was younger, I was such a people pleaser that I would "yes" myself into total exhaustion. But after I was married, Richard said something simple yet profound that has stayed with me to this day: "Lindsay, if you are going to be a doormat, you're going to get walked on."

After that, I asked the Holy Spirit to help me develop discernment concerning when to say yes and when to say no. First Samuel 30:8 says, *"David inquired of the* LORD." And God answered him. In that particular case, God said yes. David obeyed and was blessed as a result. Sometimes, though, God says no. For example, we could inquire of the Lord about a particular purchase and feel led to wait. We could inquire about a relationship or job opportunity and sense Him telling us not to pursue it. When I am unsure whether to go forward or not in a situation, the best thing I can do is "inquire of the Lord." If the answer is no, I realize that not everyone will be thrilled. But I believe God will bless our obedience.

SAYING NO CAN KEEP YOU STRONG

I believe strong godly women have learned that God doesn't always direct them to say yes to every opportunity, every invitation, and everyone. No matter what strengths a person has, strength, like a muscle, can be developed. Sometimes answering no is the best quality decision we can make. Strong godly women learn that it's okay to say no, and learn when to say it.

SOMETIMES STRONG WOMEN SAY NOTHING AT ALL

Have you ever heard the term "a deafening silence"? It's interesting because of its irony. We think of something deafening as being so loud it may shake the walls or make you want to plug your ears. Yet silence isn't loud in that way. A deafening silence is loud, so to speak, in that it captures your attention. It communicates a lot without any noise at all.

Strong godly women learn when to be quiet and not use words at all. Sometimes the wise way to defuse a situation or get it where it needs to be is to withhold a comment or refrain from saying anything. My mother-in-law, Evelyn Roberts, was a master at knowing when to keep quiet, and she had the strength and discipline to do it.

Being the wife of someone in the spotlight was always difficult for Evelyn. So many situations required that she speak up when she was uncomfortable doing so, but she knew the Lord was asking her to speak. Other situations required her to say nothing when, in my personal opinion, something needed to be said. When Oral used to joke about uncomfortable situations, he would turn to me, and, without cracking a smile, would simply say, "Something needs to be said."

As a child, keeping quiet was just part of my nature. But once I married into the Roberts family, there were many times I wanted to speak, and many times I wanted to be silent, and it took the leading of the Holy Spirit to know what to do at the time. My mother-in-law was such a great teacher of how to behave properly in difficult situations. Many times, I thought she should lose her cool, but she didn't. Many times, I thought she should say nothing, and yet she came up with the perfect thing to say. Evelyn was human, but those of us who knew her were convinced that she had a unique communication system with heaven. As she listened to the leading of the Holy Spirit, I saw her make the right quality decisions more often than not.

One of the most memorable experiences I still think about was when a person cut Evelyn off on the road. Oral, Richard, and I were all with her in the car, going to film a television program, when this person came speeding up out of nowhere, driving recklessly and making unnecessary hand gestures and comments. Evelyn was cool and calm and simply maintained her composure, and we safely got to where we were going. When I asked her why she hadn't said or done something in reaction, she was still silent. Knowing this was not the time nor the place to ask her about the situation, I simply waited until she was ready to talk to me about it.

Several days later, she addressed the situation by asking me, "Do you know why I had to keep my composure and not react in any way at all whatsoever?"

I said, "No. What was going through your thoughts at that time?"

With complete and total composure, Evelyn simply responded, "I could not afford to react to someone acting so ridiculously. I had to take care of Oral. I had precious cargo on board, and I had to take care of him."

Talk about knowing your priorities. Evelyn was not one to react—she was one to respond. And as much as I could tell, she would respond the way the Holy Spirit led her, which sometimes meant saying nothing at all.

The value of silence has been observed through the years. I have often heard this ancient saying in its English translation: "Silence is golden." An unknown author said, "Wise men speak because they have something to say; fools because they have to say something." The Roman poet Decimius Magnus Ausonius said, "He who does not know how to be silent will not know how to speak."[1] Exodus 14:14 says, *"The LORD will fight for you, and you have only to be silent"* (ESV). The *Amplified Bible* states this verse in this way: *"The LORD will fight for you while you [only need to] keep silent and remain calm."*

SILENCE IS GOLDEN—EXCEPT WHEN IT'S NOT

As valuable as silence can be, I don't want to leave this chapter without saying that there are times when silence damages a relationship or situation. Some people choose not to engage in difficult conversations that need to happen. Sometimes people do need a time-out to collect their thoughts. So I believe that with God's help, we can realize that a period of silence may just be the thing a situation needs. God's wisdom can let us know when something is better left unsaid, when silence is golden and when it's not. When you need to know whether to speak or not, ask God to direct you.

While silence may appear to be a form of weakness or a lack of knowledge about a situation, it may in fact be a sign of strength.

THE BIG QUESTION

In this chapter, you have read about saying yes, saying no, and saying nothing at all. But the big question is *when* to say what you need to say or not say anything. How can you tell when the time is right for a positive response, a negative response, or no response? For me, it comes down to what the Bible calls the *"still small voice"* of God (1 Kings 19:11–13). So often, when I need God's direction, I wait for fireworks and resounding words booming from heaven. Yet this Scripture reminds us that God also speaks in a still small voice, by His Holy Spirit.

Romans 8:16 says, *"The Spirit Himself bears witness with our spirit that we are children of God."* When God, our Father, speaks to us, something deep inside of us (our spirit) bears witness (lets us know) that God is speaking. The world might call this a gut instinct, but I call it God whispering to our inmost being to guide, guard, and direct us.

When you need to know what to say and when to say it—or not—I encourage you to pray, get quiet before the Lord, and listen for His still small voice bearing witness with your spirit. God knows the beginning from the end (Isaiah 46:10), and I believe our success is His heart's desire. While we might not get it right every time, I believe we can listen and learn and become keenly aware of when the Holy Spirit is guiding us as we speak or choose to keep silent.

SUMMARY

1. Ponder the question "Can you remain strong by saying yes to every opportunity, every invitation, and everyone who asks for something?" Strength can be developed like a muscle, and growing stronger involves making quality decisions. Sometimes answering no is the best quality decision you can make. Strong godly women discover that it's okay to say yes, to say no, or to stay silent and ask God when to say the proper response.

2. As valuable as silence can be, there are times when it can be damaging to a situation. Engaging in constant communication with God through prayer can help you develop the discipline to know whether to speak or not.

3. When God speaks to you, something deep inside you (your spirit) bears witness (lets you know) that God is speaking (Romans 8:16). The next step usually requires acting appropriately on what God has now instructed you to do.

NOTES TO SELF

Now that you've read this chapter, what notes would you like to write to yourself to help you remember the strength-building points that are most helpful to you or that apply to a specific situation in your life?

_____

_____

_____

_____

_____

9

STRONG WOMEN LISTEN

My dear brothers and sisters, take note of this:
Everyone should be quick to listen,
slow to speak and slow to become angry.
—James 1:19 (NIV)

One of the funniest experiences I've had as a mother of three daughters was when my youngest daughter, Chloe, quoted one of Oral's classic sayings with impeccable timing to get herself out of a heap of trouble.

As I was believing God for a particular need in my life, I sensed that I should speak over myself, "I am the healed of the Lord." Oral caught on to what I was saying and began to say it everywhere he went—at home, at the office, in meetings, and while he was preaching. Those seven words somehow became part of his everyday conversation.

Chloe was about six years old at the time and tiny for her age. Yet she never let that get in the way of her big personality. There was something very mature about her understanding of God and her ability to carry on an adult conversation as a child. Sometimes Chloe got into conversations with me that logically and analytically made more sense than most of my adult conversations. At times, when she needed to be disciplined, I even allowed her to decide what would be fair for a particular situation. Amazingly, she made good, reasonable choices about how to keep herself on track. As a mother, I was not only impressed but also entertained by this. I often had to turn and walk out of the room so as not to chuckle and lose the opportunity to teach her a lesson she needed to learn.

Chloe loved spending time with her grandfather and had some of the deepest conversations with him that you could imagine a small child and an evangelist having. I'm sure she heard Oral say, "I am the healed of the Lord" on many occasions. On this particular day, Chloe had just returned home from spending time with Oral and did not want to eat dinner or get ready for bed. My attempt to let her know her attitude needed to be adjusted turned into a comedy fueled by her sharp wit. I started to say, "Chloe, I am not happy with your attitude," but I paused after saying "I" just long enough for her to jump in and interject, "...am the healed of the Lord."

Because of her perfect timing, adorable little face, and tiny little hand on her tiny little hip, I doubled over with laughter. All I could say was, "Why, yes, you are!" The teaching moment vanished, and any chance of discipline went out the window.

I had to admit there was something remarkable about her quick response when she realized I was about to correct her. Her timing was perfect, for sure, but what struck me most was the realization of how closely she had been paying attention to what the adults around her were speaking. She was listening to every word. The essence of what the Bible teaches about Jesus going to the cross so that we will be healed (Isaiah 53:5) got into Chloe's little spirit, and even into her little thinking process, allowing her to make a big statement of faith.

Although I was trying to correct her, I immediately recognized this was a beautiful Proverbs 22:6 moment: *"Train up a child*

in the way he should go, and when he is old he will not depart from it."
This is one of the most important Scriptures I could ever learn and
pass on to my daughters. To this day, years later, when situations
pop up and a faith declaration is called for, I am surprised at how
often my daughters say, "I am the healed of the Lord."

Sometimes, when we don't realize the impact of what we say,
and we think no one is listening, God surprises us with situations
like what happened with Chloe. This taught me to be very careful
about my words because not only was Chloe listening with her
ears, she was listening with her spirit.

Over the years, I've discovered that the strong women I've
encountered learn to listen with their ears and with their hearts.
When they hear wisdom or something that gives them confidence,
they don't simply remember it; they believe in it and act on it. They
listen to the Word of God, to the insights of wise friends and col-
leagues, and even to the truths uttered by children. They realize
they can learn from and be strengthened by many different voices,
so they keep their ears and their hearts open in every situation.

> OVER THE YEARS, I'VE DISCOVERED THAT THE
> STRONG WOMEN I'VE ENCOUNTERED LEARN TO
> LISTEN WITH THEIR EARS AND WITH
> THEIR HEARTS.

ACTIVE LISTENING

You may have heard the term "active listening," which is simply
an expression that describes attentive and engaged listening for
both the listener and the speaker. In our society, it's easy to hear
an entire story being told by the person we are with and never stop
scrolling on our phones. Active listening is more than being physically present in someone else's company; it's engaging your heart
and mind with what the speaker is saying. It's taking what you

hear, processing it, and then choosing how to respond to the information you absorb. Active listening often creates action.

According to Mind Tools, there are five steps to effective active listening:

1. Pay attention by giving the speaker your undivided attention and looking at them directly.

2. Show that you are listening by nodding occasionally and making small verbal responses to encourage them.

3. Provide practical feedback and gain clarity by reflecting back what the speaker is saying, paraphrasing their words, and asking questions to increase your understanding.

4. Defer judgment and don't interrupt with counterarguments.

5. Respond to the speaker appropriately and respectfully. Treat them the way you think they would want to be treated.[1]

TWO QUEENS

I believe that if there is ever a time to adopt the behavior of a sponge and simply sit and soak up what's around us, it's when we are in the presence of greatness. Your personal definition of greatness may vary from the definitions of those around you. For decades, I have watched, listened to, and learned from two influential women who have had a tremendous effect on my way of approaching life. These two women, both of whom come to mind when I think of greatness, are Queen Elizabeth II and my mother-in-law, Evelyn Roberts. In many ways, they could not have been more different. But they both inspired my greatest respect, and, when they spoke, I listened intently.

ACTIVE LISTENING IS MORE
THAN BEING PHYSICALLY
PRESENT IN SOMEONE
ELSE'S COMPANY; IT'S
ENGAGING YOUR HEART
AND MIND WITH WHAT THE
SPEAKER IS SAYING.

QUEEN ELIZABETH II

Jesus Christ lived obscurely for most of his life, and never travelled far. He was maligned and rejected by many, though he had done no wrong. And yet, billions of people now follow his teaching and find in him the guiding light for their lives. I am one of them because Christ's example helps me see the value of doing small things with great love....   —Queen Elizabeth II[2]

It seems obvious that Queen Elizabeth II would command the respect of any smart listener. She served seventy years on the throne, and from the beginning of her reign, she spoke articulately, powerfully. Even though her speech was formal, I have always felt it came from the heart. After the abdication of her uncle Edward VIII in 1936, her father became King George VI. As the second son of King George V, he had not been expected to ever be crowned king of England, and he was an unlikely and perhaps even reluctant leader, though brave in his willingness to perform his duty. The king ultimately became very popular among his subjects, but he died in 1952, when he was only fifty-six years old. After his death, Elizabeth ascended the throne at the young age of twenty-five, while mourning her beloved father.

This series of events began Queen Elizabeth's remarkable life as the longest-reigning monarch in England's history. And while I never had the privilege of meeting her, I believe there were important life lessons to be learned whenever this great woman of God spoke. Her life was dedicated to her service to God, her country, her fellow human beings, and her family.

And while she undoubtedly had much to say, we can learn much from noting what she chose *not* to say and observing when and where she chose to listen. In fact, her daughter-in-law Sophie, the Duchess of Edinburgh, said, "Watching the Queen in certain situations—she's a great listener. And you see her considering what people are saying and you can see the information going in, and she clearly has a great desire to learn all the time."[3]

One of the greatest lessons we can learn in life is when to speak and when to listen. When we are in the presence of great leaders such as Queen Elizabeth II, observing their ability to listen can yield lessons worth understanding and imitating for a lifetime.

EVELYN ROBERTS

Some of the greatest life lessons I've ever had the privilege of learning came from my mother-in-law. She was a woman of seemingly few words, but the words she spoke were weighty and profound. In my book *Discover Your True Worth*, I wrote about Deborah, the biblical prophetess. Deborah was an amazing woman who ruled as judge and prophesied as God's mouthpiece. Her name means "honeybee," and I said that "if Deborah was the honeybee, then Evelyn Roberts was the *queen bee*."[4]

After years of actively observing her, silently watching and processing, one of the best lessons I ever learned was to be like a sponge and absorb and learn when in the presence of her greatness. Evelyn could change the heart of her husband, Oral, a spiritual giant in my eyes, with two words: "Now, Oral." When she spoke those words, I knew to pay special attention because she was about to speak a word of wisdom or share an insight perhaps no one else had ever thought of—and certainly no one else had the insight to speak to him in that manner. Even though Oral knew some type of correction or attempt to change his perspective would follow, the words, "Now, Oral" became music to his ears, and he learned to listen carefully to them.

While Queen Elizabeth II spent seventy majestic years on the throne of England, Evelyn Roberts spent more than seventy years praying and listening in the throne room of the Most High God. As she learned, we learned—if we were willing to pay attention and absorb her great wisdom, acquired not on an actual throne but at the feet of Jesus. Knowing the art of active listening—whether to a child, a literal queen, or a queen in your heart—takes practice. But, in my experience, it's priceless.

> THE KEY TO HEARING FROM GOD IS TO LONG FOR HIS VOICE ABOVE ALL OTHERS AND TO BE WILLING TO BE STILL AND QUIET, EXPECTING AND WAITING FOR HIM TO SPEAK.

LISTENING TO GOD

> *Trust GOD from the bottom of your heart; don't try to figure out everything on your own. Listen for GOD's voice in everything you do.* (Proverbs 3:6 MSG)

As much as listening to other people is an essential and valuable skill, we can't forget that the most important voice we should be listening to is God's voice. The primary means by which we hear from Him is through His Word, but sometimes He gets our attention in other ways. The key to hearing from God is to long for His voice above all others and to be willing to be still and quiet, expecting and waiting for Him to speak. Mother Teresa of Calcutta said, "In the silence of the heart, God speaks. If you face God in prayer and silence, He will speak to you.... Souls of prayer are souls of great silence."[5]

I will never forget one time when God spoke to Richard and me—not audibly, but in our hearts—in a way we couldn't deny. We were praying and listening for the Lord concerning a meeting Richard was scheduled to conduct overseas. We typically plan such trips far in advance, and this one was no different.

Yet, once all the arrangements were made and everything appeared to be ready to go, Richard and I both felt a terrible restlessness in our spirits. We couldn't explain the feeling or figure out why we felt it. We tried to pray it away, think it away, reason it away, and yet nothing changed. We knew the Holy Spirit was telling us not to go. We don't like to cancel meetings, but we knew beyond a shadow of a doubt that the Lord had spoken and told us that the timing was wrong. We wanted to listen and obey even though we didn't understand.

Though logic and practicality would have urged us to move forward with our plans, we decided to simply obey what we sensed and heard from God, and made the necessary cancellations. Then, one by one, everyone involved began to get on board with our decision, also feeling like something wasn't right and the timing was off.

As the time approached when the meeting would have taken place, the weather in the location where it would have been held took an unusual turn, and most travel in the area was shut down. We learned that a typhoon hit the exact spot where we would have gathered!

If ever I was grateful for the God-given ability to listen to the still small voice of God, this was one of those times. God protected us, and we knew it beyond any shadow of a doubt. Listening with your ears is one thing. But listening with your spirit is completely different. I'm so grateful God gives us the opportunity to do both and to respond accordingly. *"Whether you turn to the right or to the left, your ears will hear a voice behind you, saying, 'This is the way; walk in it'"* (Isaiah 30:21 NIV).

THE BLESSINGS OF PAYING ATTENTION

Proverbs 4:20–22 says, *"My son, pay attention to what I say; turn your ear to my words. Do not let them out of your sight, keep them within your heart; for they are life to those who find them and health to one's whole body"* (NIV). I love the part of this Scripture passage that says *"pay attention."* This is such a good reminder that we have an active part to play when it comes to what we listen to in order to learn. I love having choices, and I especially appreciate the idea that giving attention to those choices, and making wise decisions, results in something as important as life and health. Listening to God's Word is more than reading it. It's paying attention to it. So often, I can read but not really pay attention or absorb anything. But this passage tells me I can listen *and* learn. And a learning experience from God's Word can have miraculous results.

As you listen, you can learn. As you learn, you can grow in strength. As you grow in strength, you can begin to succeed. As you continue to succeed, I pray you will pass on what you have heard and learned, so others can then listen, learn, grow stronger, and succeed in all that God has for them.

SUMMARY

1. To be a good listener, it's important to practice active listening. This is different from staying silent or merely being physically present while your mind is engaged elsewhere. It's taking what you hear, processing it, and choosing how to respond to the information you absorb. Active listening often creates action.

2. If ever there is a time to adopt the behavior of a sponge and soak up what's around you, it's when you are in the presence of greatness. Great women such as Queen Elizabeth II and Evelyn Roberts knew when to speak and when to listen. Once you identify great people in your own life who can serve as similar role models for

you, watch and listen intently to learn from them and follow their example.

3. Though listening to others is an essential skill, I have found that listening to God is the most important ability you can develop. God speaks through His Word, but sometimes He will speak in other ways, including through His *still small voice* (1 Kings 19:12). Whatever way God speaks, be sure to pay attention (Proverbs 4:20).

NOTES TO SELF

Now that you've read this chapter, what notes would you like to write to yourself to help you remember the strength-building points that are most helpful to you or that apply to a specific situation in your life?

_____

_____

_____

_____

_____

SUCCEEDING BY OPERATING
FROM OUR STRENGTHS
DOESN'T MEAN IGNORING
OUR WEAKNESSES OR
ALLOWING THEM TO HINDER
US; IT SIMPLY MEANS
ACCENTUATING THE POSITIVE
THINGS ABOUT OURSELVES
AND USING OUR STRONG
POINTS TO OUR ADVANTAGE.

10

STRONG WOMEN USE THEIR STRENGTHS TO SUCCEED

*Whatever you do, work at it with all your heart, as working
for the Lord, not for human masters, since you know that
you will receive an inheritance from the Lord as a reward. It
is the Lord Christ you are serving.*
—Colossians 3:23–24 (NIV)

Think about some women you consider successful. How did
they succeed? Chances are, they learned what they needed to
know, got specific training to help them prepare, worked hard, and
probably had some help along the way. That help may have come
in the form of God's grace, a mentor or consultant who offered
sound advice and wisdom, networking opportunities that someone provided, or books and resources that allowed them to continue growing their skill sets and abilities in their chosen field. I
have found that accomplished people operate from their strengths,
using them to tackle challenges and take hold of opportunities as
they pursue success.

ACCENTUATE THE POSITIVE

In a world that sometimes seems preoccupied with solving problems, we might feel people want us to focus on our weaknesses so we can get better at what we don't naturally do well. While that approach has its place, I think there are benefits to focusing on our strengths and learning how to use them to compensate for the weaknesses we may have and to broaden the reach of the things we do well. Succeeding by operating from our strengths doesn't mean ignoring our weaknesses or allowing them to hinder us; it simply means accentuating the positive things about ourselves and using our strong points to our advantage.

Perhaps one of the greatest teachers or mentors on this subject is the apostle Paul, whose young protégé was Timothy. I believe Paul helped Timothy to minimize his weaknesses and grow in his strengths. Learning to use our strengths to our advantage involves allowing wise people to know us, see our strengths and weaknesses, pray for us, and speak into our lives in helpful ways.

> *Paul, an apostle of Jesus Christ by the will of God, according to the promise of life which is in Christ Jesus, to Timothy, a beloved son: Grace, mercy, and peace from God the Father and Christ Jesus our Lord. I thank God...as without ceasing I remember you in my prayers night and day, greatly desiring to see you, being mindful of your tears, that I may be filled with joy, when I call to remembrance the genuine faith that is in you, which dwelt first in your grandmother Lois and your mother Eunice, and I am persuaded is in you also. Therefore I remind you to stir up the gift of God which is in you through the laying on of my hands. For God has not given us a spirit of fear, but of power and of love and of a sound mind.*
>
> (2 Timothy 1:1–7)

I believe Paul was teaching Timothy to look beyond what verse 7 in the *Amplified Bible* refers to as *"timidity or cowardice or fear"* and to operate in the strengths God had given him: power, love, and a sound mind. Paul made reference to the strengths Timothy had been blessed with due to the wonderful upbringing he had enjoyed in an environment of faith with his grandmother and his mother.

Paul also wrote to Timothy, *"Be diligent to present yourself approved to God, a worker who does not need to be ashamed, rightly dividing the word of truth"* (2 Timothy 2:15). If we look at this verse in light of 2 Timothy 1:1–7, I think we can say that Paul was basically reminding Timothy that while he must be diligent to develop strength and faith for himself, he should never overlook the good things that are in him because he had a heritage of faith.

I don't know whether Paul was thinking in terms of strengths and weaknesses when he wrote to Timothy, but his message to this young man reads that way to me. At times, like Timothy, I struggle to fully recognize and embrace my own strengths and abilities. Timothy needed Paul's friendship, history with his family, and willingness to speak truth to him in order to realize how much strength was available to him.

DUST YOUR POTENTIAL OFF THE SHELF

You may be blessed, as Timothy was, to have someone in your life who encourages you in your strengths and helps you minimize what may be seen as a weakness. If not—and even if you do—I encourage you to ask God to show you anything you might be overlooking concerning the strengths He has given you. Ask Him if there are lessons, relationships, skills, experiences, or other valuable things you may have put on the back burner that He would like to bring to the forefront.

I ENCOURAGE YOU TO ASK GOD TO SHOW YOU
ANYTHING YOU MIGHT BE OVERLOOKING
CONCERNING THE STRENGTHS HE HAS
GIVEN YOU.

While you're praying about what you may need to focus on in your life right now, ask God also to show you if there are some things currently in the forefront of your life that need to move to the back. The point is to ask God for the wisdom to know what you need to pay the most attention to and what you can pay less attention to so you don't overlook any valuable strengths you already have.

WHAT ARE YOUR STRENGTHS?

Among other definitions, the following appear in *The Oxford Pocket Dictionary of the English Language* under the entry for *strength*:

+ The quality or state of being strong, in particular: physical power and energy

+ The influence or power possessed by a person, organization, or country

+ The degree of intensity of a feeling or belief

+ A good or beneficial quality or attribute of a person or thing[1]

Reflect on these definitions and ask God to reveal to you areas of personal strength you may never have thought of before. My hope is that you will begin to identify spiritual strengths, physical strengths, emotional strengths, financial strengths, and even relational strengths and see how those strengths can become assets to help you succeed at home, at work, or anywhere else. Here is a list of words that I want you to consider as possible strengths that you may never have thought about, making note of the ones you think could *best describe yourself* by saying "I am..." before the word or phrase:

Adaptable	Gifted at teaching others
Persistent	Willing to ask for help
A problem-solver	Helpful toward others
A leader	Dedicated
Motivated	Skilled at conflict resolution
Enthusiastic	Professional in my work and conduct
Positive in my outlook	
Confident	Honest and trustworthy
Compassionate	Self-motivated
Insightful	Dependable and reliable
A clear communicator	Responsible
Diligent	Innovative and creative
A team player	Eager to accept instruction
Strong under pressure	Organized
Teachable	

List here any other strengths that come to mind:

_____

_____

_____

_____

_____

_____

> THINK ABOUT WHERE YOUR LIFE COULD GO,
> WITH GOD'S HELP, IF YOU WERE TO MAXIMIZE
> THE COMBINATION OF CHARACTERISTICS
> YOU HAVE.

Which aspects of the fruit of the Spirit, found in Galatians 5:22–23, are demonstrated in your life? Look at the list and find the ones that best describe you—these are *your* spiritual strengths.

Love	Goodness
Joy	Faithfulness
Peace	Gentleness
Patience	Self-control
Kindness	

I invite you to focus on the words that jumped off the page to you—the ones that best describe your strengths. Think about how much potential you have because you possess these qualities. Think about where your life could go, with God's help, if you were to maximize the combination of characteristics you have.

LOVELY

Perhaps you have not yet had an opportunity to display or develop your strengths effectively. I have two suggestions. *First,* ask God for opportunities to exercise the strengths He has given you, and then be looking for the right time and place to utilize them. I believe you'll love doing what God has gifted you to do. *Second,* do what David did in 1 Samuel 30:6. He *"encouraged himself in the LORD"* (KJV). You can encourage yourself with words of affirmation and begin focusing on attributes that perhaps you have not considered before.

If you feel as though you cannot identify the strengths in your life, consider asking a trusted friend, family member, or coworker what they see as your strengths. Just as Paul affirmed and encouraged Timothy in his strengths, I believe people will do this for you as you ask God to help you recognize yours.

When my daughter Olivia was in design school, the entire class had to write down one positive word or phrase that described each class member and the way they designed. For my daughter, the majority of her classmates wrote down the same word. It really meant something to her, and she realized that she had never thought of it before. The word was *lovely*.

As the entire class worked through this exercise using only positive words of affirmation for each other, people in the classroom were pleasantly surprised and even shocked at the strengths their classmates saw in them.

Based on that exercise, they were required to design something using the word or phrase that best described them. My daughter said this was one of the most enlightening and enjoyable assignments she ever had.

SEVEN Rs TOWARD SUCCESS

Once you have recognized your strengths, both those that are obvious and those that may have been dormant for a while, you can use them as stepping stones toward success. Often, in the world, the pursuit of success is viewed in a positive light. But, in certain circles, those who speak of their desire to succeed have sometimes been regarded as prideful or seen as unwilling to be content with their lot in life. Yet Scripture is full of encouragement to pursue success. (See, for example, Psalm 1:1–3; Proverbs 3:1–4; 16:3.) It's okay to have successes, and it's okay to feel good about yourself throughout the process.

I've come up with what I call "Seven Rs Toward Success," and I'd like to share them with you. Whatever your strengths are, whatever your stage in life, whatever your resources—these steps can help you use your strengths to achieve the success God has ordained for you. Let's look at each one individually to help us understand how it relates to success.

1. REJOICE

When we rejoice, we celebrate. We feel and express great joy, happiness, and delight.

As you use your strengths to help you succeed, take time to rejoice. Don't wait until you reach your goal; rejoice throughout the process. I have always encouraged myself in this way, and I encourage you to express the delight of doing what God has called you to do as you move toward the ultimate accomplishment you're aiming for. Delight in the Lord. Delight in the progress you're making and the lessons you're learning. Delight in the little things you discover on your journey to something bigger.

I remember when I was in law school, I used to get paper clips and clip every ten pages of my assignments. After each set of ten pages was successfully completed, and I removed the paper clip, I would reward myself with a treat. It might have been a piece of candy or a walk around the room, but each reward moved me closer to the finish line and somehow helped me rejoice along the way. Whatever you have to do in your life to find the joy in the journey, I encourage you to do it.

I believe God has great success in store for you. It may not look like someone else's success, and that's okay. Find out what He has for you and go after it with all your heart, using your God-given strengths to help you get there and rejoice along the way.

> DELIGHT IN THE LITTLE THINGS YOU DISCOVER
> ON YOUR JOURNEY TO SOMETHING BIGGER.

2. RECITE

To recite is to speak aloud something that you have memorized or prepared—perhaps a Scripture verse, a poem, or remarks for a social event.

For as long as I have been married to Richard, he has prayed Psalm 91 over our family. To this day, we continue to pray and recite Psalm 91 over our household, even though our daughters are grown and no longer living in our home. This recitation has become part of their daily routine. We speak these words aloud so that they are released into the atmosphere as a declaration that we are setting our day according to God's Word. It has become such a routine and important part of our day that I cannot even imagine leaving the house without speaking this declaration over our family. Whether or not you recite Psalm 91, I encourage you to begin each morning by reciting a particular Scripture to set the tone for the day.

3. REFUSE

I think we all know what it means to refuse to do something. In my case, I usually apply it to not giving up. I believe to refuse is to insist we will not do something and to remain firm in that insistence. In the context of using your strengths to achieve success, as Paul encouraged Timothy, I encourage you to keep working even if you make progress just a little bit at a time. As long as you refuse to give up, I believe you'll eventually reach your goal.

4. RESOLVE

To resolve is to "find a solution to (a problem)"; to "decide firmly on a course of action."[3] As it relates to achieving the success to which God has called you, to resolve simply means to decide firmly on a godly course of action as you move toward your goal and to stick with it as best as you can, even if it is only by declaration. Remind yourself about what I am referring to when I use the term "true strength." Again, to have true strength, according to Ephesians

6:10, is to be strong in the Lord and the power of *His* might. As you read in a previous chapter, I like to teach on how important it is to fill our thoughts with productive things that create a productive result. So rather than using your energy to be discouraged, decide to use it to strengthen your resolve to do what you are called to do.

5. RECEIVE

To receive is to "be given, presented with, or paid (something)."[4] We often think of receiving in terms of being given a gift. God has given you certain natural gifts as well as spiritual strengths. I urge you to receive all that He has for you—not only your strengths, but also instruction, advice, divine intervention, or anything else necessary to get the job done as He directs and provides.

6. REWARD

A reward is something we receive when we've done well, reached a goal, or succeeded in some way. The world has a way of rewarding people, perhaps with money, accolades, or job promotions. As you use your strengths to get across the finish line in whatever God has placed on your heart to do, let me encourage you not to wait for the world to reward your effort. Believe they will and expect them to do so, but begin each project by rewarding yourself just for getting started. Find places throughout the project where you can pat yourself on the back, encourage yourself, take a break, or do something else to say to yourself, "Good job. Let's keep going." Allow others to reward you, and, most of all, allow God to reward you. As you do this at various steps along the way, I believe you'll enjoy the journey as you move toward your goal.

7. REVISIT

To revisit is to look back at past experiences or successes, examining what worked well and what contributed to turning dreams into reality. As you navigate your journey toward success, I believe it's beneficial to take time to revisit your past achievements. Reflect on the strategies, decisions, and actions that propelled you forward and brought your aspirations to fruition. By revisiting these milestones, you can gain valuable insights into your strengths, identify effective approaches, and reaffirm your capabilities. By using what has worked well for you in the past, you can inform your future decisions, refine your strategies, leverage your strengths, and effectively pursue new goals.

Looking over past successes can also serve as a source of motivation and encouragement. It can remind you of your ability to overcome challenges, persevere in the face of obstacles, and achieve your goals. Celebrate your accomplishments and acknowledge the progress you've made along the way.

Revisiting past successes can allow you to harness the wisdom gained from previous achievements and empower you to navigate future challenges with confidence and determination.

SUMMARY

1. Strong women operate from their unique, God-given strengths. By identifying these strengths and accentuating the positive, you can use your strengths to your advantage. To best understand what your strengths are and not overlook them, ask people you know and trust to pray for you and speak into your life in this area. The apostle Paul did these things for Timothy when he encouraged him not to be afraid to use his gifts. Who is the "Paul" in your life that brings encouragement to you?

2. Whether or not you have someone to encourage you in your strengths, you always have your loving heavenly Father to ask for guidance about what those strengths are. Ask Him if there are lessons, relationships, skills, or experiences you could be using as strengths. Be sure to review the lists of possible strengths found in this chapter and take note of the words that describe you. Then pray for wisdom in how to use your strengths. Ask God for chances to utilize them, and then always look for the opportunities He brings.

3. The "Seven Rs Toward Success" can help you achieve what God has called you to do. The first step is to rejoice. Second, recite Scripture over yourself and your family. Third, refuse to be discouraged. Fourth, resolve to move toward your goal and stick with it. Fifth, receive all that God has given you to achieve success. Sixth, reward yourself along the way for a job well done. Seventh, revisit your past successes and refine your strategy as you chart a course for future success.

NOTES TO SELF

Now that you've read this chapter, what notes would you like to write to yourself to help you remember the strength-building points that are most helpful to you or that apply to a specific situation in your life?

_____

_____

_____

_____

_____

I BELIEVE YOU AND I CAN
PERCEIVE GOD'S VISION FOR
OUR LIVES AS WE READ
HIS WORD AND PRAY, SHARING
OUR HEARTS WITH
HIM AND LISTENING AS HE
SPEAKS TO US.

11

STRONG WOMEN PURSUE A CLEAR VISION FOR THEIR LIVES

When what you see in your imagination is bigger than what you see in your reality, you will begin to attract the ideas, opportunities, resources, faith and relationships necessary to pursue those dreams.
—Terri Savelle Foy[1]

Have you ever encountered a strong woman who has a clear, God-given vision for her life (meaning an understanding of His purpose and plan for her) and knows how to pursue it?

When I mention such a person, you may be thinking of a friend, a coworker, a mentor, or a leader in your church. But *you* can also be this woman—strong and focused on God's vision for your life, pursuing it with passion. You may say, "Not me. I have no idea what God's vision is for my life, and I wouldn't begin to know how to pursue it." That's why I wrote this chapter. I hope and pray that by the time you've reached the end, you'll be equipped to seek God effectively, get a glimpse of His vision for your life, and go after it.

I'd like to believe that we could just sit down, ask God to download His vision for our lives, and then run with it. But that's not usually how it happens. There is an element of timing to following God's will, and few things ever seem to move quickly enough from the moment we perceive them in our hearts to the time they manifest in our lives (Ephesians 6:12). For example, Isaiah prophesied the birth of Christ (Isaiah 7:14) seven hundred years before it happened. God revealed His plan—His vision for the Savior of mankind—and carried it out. It didn't happen immediately. But it *did* happen.

I believe you and I can perceive God's vision for our lives as we read His Word and pray, sharing our hearts with Him and listening as He speaks to us. (Please note specific ideas and encouragement for discovering your vision in the "Spiritual Strength Training" section for chapter 11 at the back of this book.) As God begins to unfold all He has for us, we can utilize several important steps to pursuing that plan and reap the rewards and blessings of obedience to it in His perfect timing.

Proverbs 27:17 says, *"As iron sharpens iron, so one person sharpens another"* (NIV). My heart's desire in this chapter is to show you how to strengthen and sharpen your vision and your giftings—to point you toward a workable plan to carry out the vision and desire of your heart to do what God has called you to do.

The ten steps that I use comprise the remainder of this chapter and are designed to help you gain a clear vision for your life—God's purpose and plan for you—as you walk in obedience to Him.

Remember, these are my ten steps. You may want to personalize them according to your own particular path to success. Many times, as I am working through different projects, I use this list as an outline and then add in elements specific to the task. You may even want to make a vision board or a specific task list to keep your steps in front of you as a reminder to keep going and press toward the goal (Philippians 3:14–15).

STEP 1: PRAY

The first step I take when trying to understand God's vision for my life is to pray that God will make His vision and purpose clear. After all, He is the one who knows exactly why He created us and what He is calling us to do. In Jeremiah 29:11, He says, *"For I know the plans I have for you,…plans to prosper you and not to harm you, plans to give you hope and a future"* (NIV). Isn't this encouraging? The way to know what God knows—in this case, His purpose for our life—is to pray and ask Him, then pay attention as He answers our prayers.

The Lord promises in Jeremiah 33:3, *"Call to me and I will answer you and tell you great and unsearchable things you do not know"* (NIV). If you don't know God's vision for your life, discovering it starts with asking Him to show it to you.

STEP 2: WRITE AND DECLARE YOUR VISION DAILY

Habakkuk 2:2 says, *"Write the vision; make it plain on tablets, so he may run who reads it"* (ESV). This is one of several biblical examples in which God gives a prophet a revelation and instructs him to write it down. In most cases, the visions prophets received were for a future time. The next verse says, *"If it seems slow, wait for it; it will surely come; it will not delay"* (verse 3 ESV). Writing down my vision is vital. It keeps it fresh in my mind so I won't forget it or lose heart for it while I wait for God to bring it to pass.

For me, the whole vision was never completely clear at once, and, if you are like me, you may see your vision unfold over time. As you grow in your understanding of it, God reveals more of its meaning to you—so keep writing.

Once you've written down your vision, begin to speak it. Ephesians 4:29 says, *"Do not let any unwholesome talk come out of your mouths, but only what is helpful for building others up according to their needs, that it may benefit those who listen"* (NIV). Speak what God has shown you about His purpose and plan for your life. If you aren't sure about it yet, simply say, "I believe God has a vision for my life and that He will help me discover it and go after it in His perfect timing."

I am convinced that one of the primary ways to accomplish what really matters is to stay committed to your goals by writing and speaking about them often, even if you only talk to yourself and God. This can help you clarify what you want, motivate you to take action, provide a filter for other opportunities, help you to overcome resistance, and enable you to see and celebrate your progress.

> ONE OF THE PRIMARY WAYS TO ACCOMPLISH
> WHAT REALLY MATTERS IS TO STAY COMMITTED
> TO YOUR GOALS BY WRITING AND SPEAKING
> ABOUT THEM OFTEN.

STEP 3: ESTABLISH A PLAN

When I want to make things happen in my life, I start by developing a plan. Without proper planning, even our best-intended efforts often end up not accomplishing what they need to achieve, and we can end up stressed out and running in circles. In order to realize our goals, we need a clear plan that identifies the important steps we should take along the way. When we know and articulate our objective, a solid plan empowers us to move forward.

God has a plan and a purpose for each one of us. We can believe it and look forward to it, but as James 2:20 says, *"faith without good deeds ["works" NKJV] is useless"* (NLT). To take your dreams and visions from your heart to your reality, you need to take action—even small steps can make a big impact on realizing your vision. Here are four steps you can take that will help you bring your hopes, dreams, and visions to life:

1. *Write down the details.* Earlier, I mentioned the importance of writing down and declaring your overall vision. Now it's time to add the specifics. In Exodus 25–27, 35–40, God laid out the plans for building the tabernacle. He didn't just give Moses a general overview; He gave him very detailed instructions. Sometimes the details make all the difference, so take time to think through the ones you need to tend to, and be sure to write them down.

2. *Identify your action steps.* Decide and write down each step you need to take to get the outcome you desire, and identify why they are needed—even the ones that seem small. Regardless of what that vision is—to be a good wife, to run a company, to run for public office, or anything else God leads you to do—make a list and check it twice. Identify a game plan so that you can stay on track.

3. *Resolve to take the specific steps needed to execute each aspect of your plan.* To resolve to do what you need to do to see your vision come to pass is to get your head and your heart aligned with it. Paul wrote, *"I press toward the goal for the prize of the upward call of God in Christ Jesus"* (Philippians 3:14). To press toward the goal is to be intentional and to go after it with resolve.

Think through each step you'll need to take and resolve (commit) to take it.

4. *Start at the beginning and stay in God's timing.* I'm a firm believer in proper, helpful shortcuts, but not shortcuts that compromise the integrity of a vision. As you pursue the vision God has given you, start at the beginning, even if it seems like a small step to take. With each step, be patient and work within God's time frame. Walk out your specific plan, in faith, one step at a time. *"The steps of a good man are ordered by the LORD, and He delights in his way"* (Psalm 37:23).

STEP 4: HAVE AN ATTITUDE OF GRATITUDE

Gratitude is one of the greatest keys to having godly plans succeed. First Thessalonians 5:18 says, *"Be thankful in all circumstances, for this is God's will for you who belong to Christ Jesus"* (NLT). Notice it does not say to be thankful *for* all circumstances, because not everything that happens is great. Yet we can give God thanks *in the midst of* all situations. Psalm 22:3 says that God inhabits (lives and dwells in) the praises of His people (KJV). As we praise Him, He has an opportunity to move in our lives. I believe God is pleased when we are thankful, so remind yourself of this Scripture and *"enter his gates with thanksgiving and his courts with praise"* (Psalm 100:4 NIV).

STEP 5: ASK GOD TO TELL YOU A SECRET

Daniel 2:20–22 says that God *"knows all, does all: ...he provides both intelligence and discernment, he opens up the depths, tells secrets,* sees in the dark—light spills out of him!" (MSG). I pray, every day, "Lord, let secret things be revealed and hidden things come out of darkness." I ask God to tell me a secret, so to speak, and I encourage you to do the same. Ask Him to show you what you need to know—even if you can't readily see it.

Sometimes what looks good on the surface turns out not to be good at all, and vice versa. As you pursue your God-given vision, it's important to know who and what you can trust. God can reveal anything you need to know, and that will keep you moving toward the vision He has given you without getting distracted or wasting effort.

STEP 6: DECLUTTER

According to *Merriam-Webster.com Dictionary, clutter* is defined as "a crowded or confused mass or collection."[2] Does that sound like a closet, garage, basement, or car you know of? Clutter reflects the opposite of what 1 Corinthians 14:33 says about God: *"For God is not the author of confusion but of peace."*

In Matthew 6:10, Jesus teaches us to pray, *"Your kingdom come. Your will be done on earth as it is in heaven."* Can you imagine heaven as a cluttered or confused mess? God is a God of balance and order, and we should do all we can to achieve and maintain balance and order, not only in our spiritual life but in our plans as well.

As I talked about in chapter 5, "Strong Women Maximize Their Mental Real Estate," I believe one of the best things we can do for our spiritual benefit is to declutter our thoughts. Our thoughts can become our belief system, and when they become our belief system, they can become the way we live. Freeing ourselves from chaos and disorder can bring us more time to pray, worship, be creative, and study God's Word—and practice being obedient to it.

Ask God to show you any area in your life that you may need to declutter.

STEP 7: SPIRITUALLY DETOXIFY

Do you ever find yourself praying, as David did in Psalm 51:10, *"Create in me a clean heart, O God, and renew a right and steadfast spirit within me"* (AMP)? David's prayer is a great example for us to follow. He was deeply committed to pleasing God and willing to take the necessary steps to align with His will.

Many people know what it means to cleanse or detoxify the physical body from something harmful. But what about our spiritual well-being? What about the worries, fears, or jealousies that can weigh down our souls?

Take a moment to ask God to reveal any areas in your spiritual life in need of detoxification. Pray and see if there is anything that is out of alignment with His character or Word. Ask God if there are any areas that you may need to renew or refresh in order to accomplish all that He has for you to do.

> THE MORE YOU READ THE BIBLE, THE MORE YOUR FAITH CAN GROW. THE MORE YOUR FAITH GROWS, THE CLOSER YOU CAN GET TO ACHIEVING YOUR GOD-GIVEN DREAM.

STEP 8: USE YOUR FAITH

As I work toward achieving my dreams, one of my biggest enemies is fear. We learn from 2 Timothy 1:7 that fear is not a spirit that comes from God. I'm not talking about the kind of healthy caution that keeps me from real dangers, but the unhealthy, ungodly kind that comes from the devil to keep me from doing what God has called me to do. The best way I can attack this kind of fear is with faith. Hebrews 11:6 tells us, *"But without faith it is impossible to please Him, for he who comes to God must believe that He is, and that He is a rewarder of those who diligently seek Him."*

Think of your faith as a muscle that God works through. How do we exercise our faith muscle? Romans 10:17 has the answer: *"Faith comes by hearing, and hearing by the word of God."* The more you read the Bible, the more your faith can grow. The more your faith grows, the closer you can get to achieving your God-given dream. Don't stop short of your miracle by giving up on your faith.

STEP 9: BE TEACHABLE

In Matthew 18:3, Jesus tells us we must become like little children to enter the kingdom of heaven. I've always seen little children as teachable. One way we can become teachable is by following God's instructions, which we find in His Word.

Here are three things I do to better follow God's instructions:

1. *Be prepared.* Renew your mind according the Word of God (Romans 12:2) and put on your spiritual armor daily (Ephesians 6:10–18).

2. *Be persistent.* Continue to obey God and wait for Him even when it doesn't seem as if His answer is coming. *"Ask and keep on asking and it will be given to you; seek and keep on seeking and you will find; knock and keep on knocking and the door will be opened to you"* (Matthew 7:7 AMP).

3. *Be committed to reaching the finish line.* Keep the goal in mind. *"Let us lay aside every weight, and the sin which so easily ensnares us, and let us run with endurance the race that is set before us"* (Hebrews 12:1).

STEP 10: REJOICE IN THE LORD

God instructs us to take joy in Him. You might say, "What if I'm having a bad day and don't feel like it?" The answer is in Philippians 4:4: *"Rejoice in the Lord **always.**"*

Happiness and joy are two different things, but both can be accomplished through prayer. Keep in mind, all the true joy and true strength I refer to in this book points back to *the* Book, the Bible. Nehemiah 8:10 says that the joy of the Lord is our strength. When we are in fellowship with God, we have access to the joy that is in Him, and His joy is what makes us strong. The joy of the Lord is one of the characteristics of Jesus (John 15:11) that we can incorporate into our daily life as we call upon Him. While some situations may not seem so cheery, as we allow the Holy Spirit to manifest joy in us as a fruit of the Spirit (Galatians 5:22), we find that we can have a joyful heart in the midst of difficult situations.

So, how does this help us achieve our dreams? Psalm 37:4 gives us the answer: *"Delight yourself also in the LORD, and He shall give you the desires of your heart."*

KEEP PUTTING ONE FOOT IN FRONT OF THE OTHER

Again, I have always found that the way to achieve the vision God has given me is to go after it one step at a time. Take one step, then another, then another. There may be times when God supernaturally downloads plans and goals and ideas all at once. But I have found that, even when that happens, I have to unpack each step one at a time. The ten steps explained in this chapter are designed to help you get started and keep you focused as you move forward. Whatever your God-given vision may be, I encourage you to pursue it according to God's plan.

SUMMARY

1. When trying to understand and fulfill God's vision for your life, consider the ten steps I use to clarify and achieve my goals, personalizing them for yourself and applying each one to your unique situation.

2. Remember, your list, your ten steps, for gaining a clear vision may be different from mine. These ten steps are meant to be used as a guide for you to glean from. I pray they will build your faith and confidence so that you can fully realize all that God has put in your heart to do.

3. Go back and review steps 1–10 and rephrase them to fit your situation as you begin to apply them.

NOTES TO SELF

Now that you've read this chapter, what notes would you like to write to yourself to help you remember the strength-building points that are most helpful to you or that apply to a specific situation in your life?

_____

_____

_____

_____

I SEE PEACE AND
FORGIVENESS AS AN ACT THAT
IS WORKED IN MY HEART
THROUGH PRAYER AND
STRENGTH IN GOD.

12

STRONG WOMEN FORGIVE

Forgiveness is an act of the will, and the will can function
regardless of the temperature of the heart.
—Corrie ten Boom[1]

This chapter was by far the hardest part of this book for me to write. It wasn't a challenge because I don't want to forgive. I always want to forgive. Writing a chapter about forgiveness was hard because I recognize how difficult it can be for a human being to forgive—especially when someone has been deeply hurt. I persevered to write it anyway because forgiveness is such a powerful, spiritually rewarding dynamic.

I want to state clearly that my forgiving someone does *not* mean I approve of what that person has done. It means I choose to let go of the pain their actions caused and move forward, trusting God to heal me and trusting God to deal with them. It means I have recognized that Jesus asks me to forgive them by giving my situation to God as an act of faith so I can be free.

PURSUE PEACE

Hebrews 12:14–15 says, *"Pursue peace with all people, and holiness, without which no one will see the Lord: looking carefully lest anyone fall short of the grace of God."* I have found that when I have strife and turmoil of any form in any relationship, it hinders my thinking and consumes more of my attention than I desire. Such strife and turmoil can take the form of unforgiveness, resentment, arguments, or any uncomfortable disagreement.

That is when I like to remember Joshua 24:15: *"**Choose** for yourselves this day whom you will serve…. But as for me and my house, we will serve the LORD."* As I wrote earlier, I love having choices, especially when they involve my life. I can choose to pursue peace. I can choose to obey the Lord, and I pray you can do the same in whatever circumstances you are going through.

> **FORGIVENESS IS AN ACT OF OBEDIENCE TO GOD;
> IT HAS A SPIRITUAL COMPONENT. THAT'S WHY
> IT CAN BE DONE AS AN ACT OF FAITH.**

In my years of ministry, I have encountered people who experienced having a spouse who committed adultery, a business partner who betrayed them, and many other hurtful scenarios that pierced their hearts. During our talks, I noticed that many people spent a lot of time and energy rehearsing what happened and speaking intensely about the situations they experienced. The situation may have happened many years ago, or the person may no longer be in their life, but their pain is still very present.

I would pray over these dear people, believing they would be able to release the circumstances that were keeping them stuck in that moment of pain. During my times of prayer, I realized forgiveness is hard for me. Even though it is for my benefit, it can sometimes feel like I'm letting the offender "off the hook." That is why I want to make sure you understand that, through Christ, *forgiveness sets us free.*

I remember a time when I was arguing with God over the action of forgiving and my ability to do so. Jesus said to me, "Do you believe I can forgive them?" I said, "Yes, You're Jesus." He replied, "Then do it through Me, and I'll give you the strength" (Philippians 4:13).

Forgiveness is an act of obedience to God; it has a spiritual component. That's why it can be done as an act of faith. Richard always says to forgive by faith until your feelings catch up with your faith. I wholeheartedly agree! Even if it only starts with my words, eventually, it gets into my heart. In no way am I talking about personally going and confronting the person or situations in my life. I am talking about going to God in prayer. Therefore, I see peace and forgiveness as an act that is worked in my heart through prayer and strength in God. I can do what God says to do many times throughout His Word: *forgive* and then pray for Father God to do what only He can do, which is to work in the situation and set me free.

Remember, God sent His Comforter, His Holy Spirit, to help us in times of need. You can ask God to give you strength and to be at work in your situation and relationships with others and to bring healing and wholeness to your life.

LITTLE FOXES SPOIL THE WHOLE VINE

One of the most unusual times the Lord required me to forgive happened in a situation that seemed to come out of the blue. I believe that one of God's favorite places to dwell in is in the land of "out of the blue."

I was struggling with a really mean-spirited person who called himself a Christian. I felt he was about half on God's team and half on the devil's starting lineup. I had to practice forgiveness on a regular basis because his attacks against my family were constant and relentless. I often wondered what his motive was, but my best answer was that he simply allowed the devil to use him as his messenger.

On a day when I sincerely struggled with forgiving his latest attack, I found myself almost obsessing over mustard. As strange as that sounds, I looked down to see a tiny spot of mustard on my white shirt. The spot commanded my total focus, and I just couldn't get past it. The other 99 percent of my shirt was nice and white, but that one spot got the best of me.

As I wondered why I was so focused on this mustard spot, I remembered Ephesians 5:27 where Paul talks about *"not having spot or wrinkle or any such thing."* As that verse stayed on my mind, my thought was, "Why did those words pop into my head? Why now? And what does that have to do with mustard?" None of it seemed to have anything at all to do with the pain of the situation I was going through.

But it was as if the Holy Spirit was whispering the sweetest thought to me, helping me understand that while rest of the shirt was fine, the stain had to be dealt with. Not only was the mustard spot all that I had been focusing on, but my awareness of it had caused people around me to focus on it too. Not one of us was talking about the shirt, just the stain!

Immediately, I thought of the situation with the man who seemed so determined to hurt my family. I had so many lovely things in my life. My life was okay, but the stain of my choosing unforgiveness was there. In spite of my many blessings, unforgiveness appeared to be the main focus of my thoughts and of my conversations with God. Needless to say, I got the point; I had to deal with the issue of unforgiveness and let God wash me *"white as snow"* (Isaiah 1:18).

Song of Solomon 2:15 says, *"Catch for us the foxes, the little foxes that ruin the vineyards, our vineyards that are in bloom"* (NIV). This verse teaches us that it's not only the big situations in life that cause us trouble—it's also the little things we may overlook. I believe Satan takes great joy in distracting us with the "little foxes" in order to separate us from God's highest and best for our lives.

But I also believe that if we are filled with the Spirit of God, there is little room for the enemy's tricks and strategies (Ephesians 6:11).

JESUS, OUR EXAMPLE

The greatest act of ultimate sacrifice happened two thousand years ago when Jesus went to the cross to purchase our salvation, our healing, and our right relationship with God so we can live an eternal and everlasting life with Him.

As the Roman soldiers crucified Jesus, He said, *"Father, forgive them, for they do not know what they are doing"* (Luke 23:34 NIV, NRSV). This sinless Man, taking on the sins of the world and speaking His last few sentences on earth, said, in agony, *"Forgive."* And if Jesus, who *"knew no sin"* (2 Corinthians 5:21), could forgive, so can I through Christ who gives me strength (Philippians 4:13).

Let me reiterate: forgiving someone doesn't mean I approve of their wrong behavior. By releasing them (forgiving them), I am simply giving them over to God and allowing Him to handle the situation, while I keep my thoughts, my emotions, and my spirit free.

LET'S PRAY

I would like to pray for you.

> I pray for God to set you free from any harm or hurt or suffering that has caused you pain. I pray for you and encourage you to release anything from your spirit and soul that would hinder your progress in moving forward. As you trust God, I ask Him to bless you, to heal you, and to set you on a path of total and complete wholeness, joy, success, and prosperity in every aspect of your life. In Jesus's name, amen.

SUMMARY

1. Review key Scriptures from this chapter, such as these:

   Pursue peace with all people, and holiness, without which no one will see the Lord. (Hebrews 12:14)

   Choose for yourselves this day whom you will serve.... But as for me and my house, we will serve the LORD. (Joshua 24:15)

   Catch for us the foxes, the little foxes that ruin the vineyards, our vineyards that are in bloom. (Song of Solomon 2:15 NIV)

2. Review what Jesus did on the cross when He said, "*Father, forgive them, for they do not know what they are doing*" (Luke 23:34 NIV, NRSV).

3. Now, go back and reread my prayer for you.

NOTES TO SELF

Now that you've read this chapter, what notes would you like to write to yourself to help you remember the strength-building points that are most helpful to you or that apply to a specific situation in your life?

_____

_____

_____

_____

_____

NO MATTER WHAT
SEASON OF LIFE WE ARE
IN, WE ARE ALWAYS ON THE
WINNING TEAM WHEN WE
WALK WITH GOD.

13

STRONG WOMEN KNOW WHEN TO MOVE ON

You will be blessed when you come in and
blessed when you go out.
—Deuteronomy 28:6 (NIV)

In chapter 4, "Strong Women Go to the Ball," we talked about Cinderella. Let's think about her story again. While this is a fairy tale and not something on which I would base my Christian life, I find that a particular principle in this story is something to pay attention to. Remember that, given her natural circumstances, there was no chance Cinderella could go to the ball. But her fairy godmother appeared, turned a pumpkin into a coach, arrayed her with a beautiful ball gown and a pair of glass slippers, and—voila! Off she went to the ball to have the time of her life. Her fine gifts came with a warning: the splendor would wear off at midnight.

Had she not left the ball on time, the prince would have seen her as she really was—a poor working girl in a tattered dress, with old shoes and a pumpkin. Cinderella was aware that timing was important on this special night, and she left the ball when she was supposed to—accidentally leaving behind a glass slipper that ultimately led to the search that destined her to be a queen. Thank God for the right pair of shoes!

Again, while I don't choose to live my life according to storybooks, I believe there are a couple of important concepts here: timing is everything, and some things should be left in the past. Sometimes what we leave behind us opens the door to greater successes in our future. Strong godly women develop a sensitivity to God's timing as He unfolds the destiny He has purposed for them.

THERE'S NOT A FAIRY GODMOTHER OR A DEADLINE

Sometimes I think Cinderella had it easy because she knew the exact moment she should make her exit. As a general rule, we don't always have such clear instructions. While I'm certain that many blessings await us on the other side of our "Exit" doors, we don't always know when and how to walk through them. Some women cut and run because the going gets tough, when they should stay longer. Other times, they stay when they really need to walk away.

Have you ever stayed in a job, ministry, association, or friendship too long, well past the time when you should have ended things?

> STRONG GODLY WOMEN DEVELOP A SENSITIVITY TO GOD'S TIMING AS HE UNFOLDS THE DESTINY HE HAS PURPOSED FOR THEM.

How many of us have hung on to a job when all signs told us we should move on? Maybe there's a merger, a corporate sale, or a management change, and we see the "writing on the wall" that our position is in jeopardy. Yet we might stay until they show us the door. Sometimes we end up staying in our position out of guilt and fear, but our heart is no longer in it. Have you ever seen people who do what the business world calls "quiet quitting," where they just do the bare minimum to get by?

We don't have a fairy godmother to tell us what to do, solve our problems, or give us "midnight curfews" that usher us to the exit doors we should take in our lives. So how do we know when it's time to move on? Let me share some examples of how other people have discerned when to make a well-timed and God-honoring exit.

A GRACIOUS EXIT LEADS TO BLESSINGS

In Genesis 13, Abram (before God changed his name to Abraham) and his nephew Lot were living together in Bethel. By then, Abram had become quite wealthy in livestock, and Lot had herds as well. After a while, *"the land could not support them while they stayed together, for their possessions were so great that they were not able to stay together. And quarreling arose between Abram's herders and Lot's"* (verses 6–7 NIV).

Abram was wise enough to see that it was time for them to go their separate ways. He said to Lot, *"Let's not have any quarreling between you and me, or between your herders and mine, for we are close relatives. Is not the whole land before you? Let's part company. If you go to the left, I'll go to the right; if you go to the right, I'll go to the left"* (verses 8–9 NIV).

In letting Lot choose first, Abram showed grace and humility and didn't demand the best land for himself. Interestingly, Lot chose the most beautiful-looking land near the Jordan River, which turned out to be adjacent to the cities of Sodom and Gomorrah. I'm sure that could be a lesson in itself about how something that looks good on the surface may not always be the best—ultimately, both cities were destroyed because of the sin of the people who lived in them.

Meanwhile, Abram went to live near Hebron. That's where God met him, called him into a powerful covenant, gave him the miracle of a son in his old age, and made him the father of many nations (Genesis 15, 17). So the lesson in this story is this: if you follow where God leads you, and you do it in His timing, you position yourself for Him to meet you there and bless you.

> SOMETIMES THE HOLY SPIRIT BREAKS THROUGH SUDDENLY IN A SITUATION AND CHANGES THE DIRECTION IN WHICH WE ARE HEADED.

MOVING ON IN GOD'S PERFECT TIMING

Ecclesiastes 3:1 says, *"To everything there is a season, a time for every purpose under heaven."* In other words, timing often has a lot to do with results. Sometimes the only difference between a positive result and a negative one is the timing of events and the decisions leading up to it. Opportunities that require choosing whether to stay in a situation or move on often present themselves, so it's important for us to seek God, stay prayerful, and follow the direction in which the Holy Spirit leads.

Sometimes the Holy Spirit breaks through suddenly in a situation and changes the direction in which we are headed. This very thing happened to my father-in-law, Oral, while he was a student in college. One day, the professor said, "It is a scientific impossibility for a woman to have been made from Adam's rib." This was said at a Christian college! Oral could not understand what was happening. Frustrated and not really knowing what to do or how to comment, he just sat there. He wanted to be respectful, but, at the same time, it didn't make any sense to him that a Christian faculty member in a sociology class would make such a statement.

Oral was a young, newly saved Christian who had been raised in a Christian home. He had been healed of tuberculosis by the power of God. But now he was being presented with teaching that seemed to deny God's supernatural power. As he sat quietly in a classroom filled with seemingly confused students, the Lord unmistakably led him to get up and leave. While some people might have been cautious about making a scene by leaving, Oral wasn't. He got up, and, as he was walking out, he felt an even stronger voice in his heart say, "Don't be like other men. Be like Jesus and heal the people."

Immediately, Oral knew that one season in his life was over and another was about to begin. Imagine if he had simply stayed in the classroom in that discontented state and done nothing. But when you understand the nudging, the prompting, of the Holy Spirit, you can discern when to stay and when to go. Oral had not been planning to change anything about his life or his schooling, but, at that time, God desired to change it. Here we see once again that timing is critical. And the results of obedience spoke volumes.

MOVING ON TO A CHAMPIONSHIP

This next story is not in the Bible, and neither are any of the people in it Bible characters. However, I believe I can learn from reading about well-implemented plans that result in an amazing success story. So as I gleaned from this story, I pray you can too.

I have been a Detroit Tigers fan since I was a child, and to this day, the Tigers remain my favorite baseball team. My happiest childhood memories are of sitting in their stadium. That's why I often see correlations between baseball and spiritual things.

Let's look at perhaps the most memorable trade in Tigers' baseball history—certainly the most memorable one I've ever seen. It's also one of the best examples I've ever seen of knowing when to move on.

In August 2017, the Tigers were near the end of a losing season when pitcher Justin Verlander was given the opportunity to be traded to the Houston Astros. After being with the team for twelve years, this wasn't an easy decision for him, but he decided it was time to move on.

In his farewell speech, Verlander noted that he'd had about forty-five minutes to make the hardest decision of his life. He went on to say that he had learned from other athletes in similar situations the importance of making strategic entrances and strategic exits—and to make them with dignity. He observed that this is true not only in sports, but in all kinds of situations.[1]

Just two months after Verlander left Detroit to play for Houston, the Astros won the World Series. Imagine being a sports hero in the city where you had played for twelve years, playing for a team in last place, and then, in a matter of months, helping to win the World Series with the number-one team in Major League Baseball.

How did this happen? Well, I'd say it took an enormous amount of talent and perhaps a miracle. I have to believe that if Justin Verlander could go from being on the worst team in the league to playing on the team that won the World Series, things can change quickly for us too. I believe in miracles, and I am confident that, as children of the Most High God, we can experience unusual and immediate changes that move us from defeat to the greatest victory.

In my observation, not every change God leads us to make will happen quickly, but some changes do. One day, we're on the metaphoric losing team, and our lives may seem dismal or even hopeless. The next day, we are on the winning team, and our dreams are being fulfilled. In truth, though, no matter what season of life we are in, we are always on the winning team when we walk with God.

A GRACE-FILLED GOODBYE

I once had a friend who approached every situation with negativity. Each time we were together, I felt heavier afterward. After much prayer, I felt led to discontinue the relationship in the most gracious manner I could think of—to pray for her and to bless her as we went our separate ways. It was difficult because the way she treated me was unkind, and, in the flesh, I wanted to correct the lies she was telling others about me. But I continued to remind myself of what I had heard in my time of prayer—to bless her and separate.

I later discovered that she was treating other people in the same negative ways she had treated me. While I should have been happy that I had released the relationship when I was supposed to, I was actually bothered by it. I asked God a ridiculous question: "Why did I have to treat her so well at the end of our relationship?"

His answer was interesting. I felt that He said to me, "While you don't need her as a friend, I don't want you to make an enemy of her." I had never thought of that. I haven't dealt with that person since then, but, again, I know I did my best to handle the situation with grace. We may never know the pain we were spared in our obedience to leave when we listen to the promptings and warnings of our spirit.

Sometimes we have to move on in our employment or our friendships or other relationships. Sometimes we have to let others move on. But, at all times, God can help us go forward as painlessly as possible when we pray and listen to Him. Even if the other person does not respond as we had hoped, God still can give us the grace we need.

THE MOST IMPORTANT MOVING ON OF ALL TIME

It is to your advantage that I go away; for if I do not go away, the Helper will not come to you; but if I depart, I will send Him to you. (John 16:7)

To me, Bible history's most important story of moving on is described in John 16 and 17, when Jesus prepares to go to the cross after being in public ministry for only about three years. In chapter 17, Jesus speaks directly with His Father about His return to heaven and prays for His disciples and for all current and future believers.

This is one of my favorite chapters in the Bible because it explains Jesus's power and authority and shows His conscious decision to pass on that power and authority to believers after He leaves earth and ascends to heaven. His departure was well thought out, well planned, well documented, and well executed—it was fully complete. Because the Lord Jesus was willing to leave His heavenly home to come to earth, we get to see and experience the goodness of God. Because He was willing to leave His earthly life and return to the Father, we get to have the Holy Spirit, the Comforter, to minister to us at all times.

In John 14:9, Jesus says that if we've seen Him, we've seen the Father. The biblical accounts of Jesus's presence on earth give us insights into the love and goodness of God in such a visual way that we can clearly see who God is and how much He cares for us. Then Jesus explains that He has already planned ahead for us by promising to send the Holy Spirit, the divine Helper called to come alongside us, following His departure (verse 26). Not only that, but He also says He is going ahead to prepare places for us in our eternal home (verse 3). So not only was He moving on, but He was planning ahead for the day you and I would move on as well!

Every time I think of how difficult things can be in my life, I remember Jesus's willingness to move from heaven to earth—and His willingness to later move from earth back to heaven. These reminders keep me grounded as I seek to follow God's leading in and out of life's various seasons and opportunities.

I pray, as you focus on the example Jesus set for us, that every time God leads you to move on, you will do so with God's grace and timing. The choices you make are important. Metaphorically speaking, it's vital that you stay at the ball long enough to be introduced to your destiny, but not so long that you miss your exit window. I believe the more closely we follow the Holy Spirit's leading as we walk through life, the more we can operate in obedience from a position of strength and great joy.

SUMMARY

1. Often, some of the best things in life are waiting for us after we've left something behind. The strong godly women I have observed develop a sense of when to stay and when to move on, a sensitivity to God's timing. Ecclesiastes 3:1 says, *"To everything there is a season, a time for every purpose under heaven."* Sometimes the only difference between having a result that is positive and one that isn't is the timing of the events and the decisions leading up to it. That's why it's important for us to seek God, stay prayerful, and follow the direction in which the Holy Spirit leads.

2. In my observation, not every change God leads us to make will happen quickly, but some changes do. One day, we're metaphorically on the losing team, and our life may seem stuck. The next day, we're on the winning team, and our dreams are being fulfilled. But whether changes happen slowly or suddenly, trust God with the outcome and His perfect timing.

3. Every time I think about how difficult things can be in my life, I remember Jesus's willingness to move from heaven to earth—and His willingness to later move

from earth back to heaven. These reminders keep me grounded as I seek to follow God as He leads me in and out of life's seasons and opportunities. I encourage you to again focus on Ecclesiastes 3:1 and allow God to speak to your heart. By doing so, you can gain a deeper understanding of God's timing and how it relates to the particular seasons of your life.

NOTES TO SELF

Now that you've read this chapter, what notes would you like to write to yourself to help you remember the strength-building points that are most helpful to you or that apply to a specific situation in your life?

_____

_____

_____

_____

_____

14

STRONG WOMEN BOUNCE BACK

When you are feeling the sting of a setback,
God is preparing you for your comeback.
—Tim Storey[1]

As I pay close attention to the characteristics of strong godly women, I consistently observe a key quality: resilience. I define resilience as the ability to bounce back after a significant setback. Most people are going to come across a few bumps in the road, but a resilient person will address the issues and get back on course. I realize that bumps in the road, or setbacks, can come in many different shapes and sizes. A setback doesn't have to keep you back. I find that thought encouraging because it shows me that not every situation in my life has to be tiptoe-through-the-tulips perfect.

Isaiah 43:18–19 says, *"Forget the former things; do not dwell on the past. See, I am doing a new thing! Now it springs up; do you not perceive it? I am making a way in the wilderness and streams in the wasteland"* (NIV). These verses encourage letting go of the past, when necessary, and embracing the new things that God is doing. They speak of God's ability to bring about transformation and renewal, even in the most unlikely or difficult circumstances.

They're a reminder to keep faith and trust in God's plan for the future no matter what comes your way.

Letting go of the past, as needed, and embracing the future can feel challenging. Loss can strike a friendship, a marriage, a person's finances, someone's dreams, a spouse, or even a child, which is what happened to me. I felt broken. But God's desire for me was not to stay in devastation—it was for restoration. I had to stand on God's promises in Isaiah 43 that God had new things in store for me. Through my own journey of healing and resilience, I have been able to minister to others who were dealing with deeply hurtful situations. This decision to do a new thing is not easy, but it's biblical. I have found that many women need to make the same decision to press forward into a new thing in some area of their life. I want to encourage those who feel stuck in their past to reread Isaiah 43. I believe you can spring into a fresh start and do so without hesitation or guilt.

LIGHTEN THE LOAD

I have a friend who lives in Detroit, Michigan, and every year, we have a conversation about the snowstorms that wreak havoc there throughout the winter months. We remember the stories of cars (including our own) being stuck in past blizzards and what we've seen drivers do to get moving again. Most often, the passengers got out of the car to lighten the load while the driver attempted every possible smart and not-so-smart maneuver to get the vehicle unstuck from the snowdrift. But the comedy we observed on more occasions than we could count was how the driver would take off on the open road once they had cleared the drift, leaving the passengers behind. And, yes, I was once a stranded passenger left in the cold, and the driver had to come back and get me!

Although our winter-weather stories represent a lot of funny and happy memories for us both, I see an amazing life lesson when I think about the need for drivers to lighten the load in order to go forward. One of the most unusual stories I heard was about a truck driver who was driving under a bridge and thought he could clear it with enough space above. Unfortunately, he was wrong, and he scraped the underside of the concrete bridge with the top of his truck, ultimately getting wedged and bringing traffic to a stand-still. As traffic piled up behind him and tempers became short, the observers tried to figure out a way to get the truck loose and the traffic moving. After hours with no solution, a little boy came walking up with his father and said something like, "Hey, mister, why don't you let some air out of the tires?" This out-of-the-mouth-of-babes statement saved the day. The truck driver was able to let just enough air out of the tires to fit under the bridge and move on.

> AS WE TRAVEL THROUGH LIFE, THERE WILL BE
> TIMES WHEN WE HAVE TO ASSESS, EVALUATE,
> AND DETERMINE JUST WHAT WE SHOULD HOLD
> ON TO AND WHAT WE NEED TO LET GO OF.

The truck driver hadn't intended to get his truck stuck under the bridge, but things happen—good things and bad things. Sometimes it's hard to move forward from the past because it's so wonderful. Sometimes it's hard to move forward from the past because it's so painful. Either way, if you're stuck in the past, in a rut, like the cars in the snowdrift or the 18-wheeler under the bridge, and can't move forward, I believe there's no time like now to get unstuck. Sometimes the only solution to being released to move forward is to lighten the load. So when you hit a setback, a rut in the road, consider looking for areas in your life where you can release the past. Ask God to reveal anything that might be holding you back.

I like to be as prepared as possible for the "bumps" in the road of life (this was especially so when I was younger and traveled over-seas). The one thing a seasoned traveler knows is to travel light. Excess baggage is not only difficult to carry around, but it can be costly in other ways as well. It is important to pare down to the essentials that are necessary for the journey. As we travel through life, there will be times when we have to assess, evaluate, and determine just what we should hold on to and what we need to let go of.

CRAWL, WALK, RUN, OR ROLLER-SKATE

Hebrews 12:1–3 talks about the race of endurance that believers run and how we can learn from those who have successfully run it before us. In *The Message*, this passage says:

> *We'd better get on with it..., start running—and never quit!... Keep your eyes on **Jesus**, who both began and finished this race we're in. Study how he did it. Because he never lost sight of where he was headed—that exhilarating finish in and with God—he could put up with anything along the way: Cross, shame, whatever. And now he's **there**, in the place of honor, right alongside God. When you find yourselves flagging in your faith, go over that story again, item by item, that long litany of hostility he plowed through. **That** will shoot adrenaline into your souls!* (emphases are in the original)

As you navigate your way to godly strength and success, only you can decide how you get to your destination—you can crawl, walk, run, roller-skate, ride a scooter, or take a bus. Whatever it is, only you can choose how you move forward. No matter how you decide to do it, I encourage you to go. Start the journey. A long walk starts with one step. A long drive starts with one block. Counting to one million starts with the number one. Although sometimes I'd prefer to start at the finish line, life doesn't work that way. I have to picture the finish line in my mind to know what I'm looking forward to, but I still have to start at the beginning. In fact, the first book of the Bible, Genesis, starts with the words, *"In the beginning"* (verse 1). In my experience, there's a beginning, a middle, and an end to most things. But I can't get to the middle or the end if I don't start at the beginning. Even Julie Andrews, in her role as Maria in the *Sound of Music,* sang that the "very beginning" is "a very good place to start"![2]

Because I like to see the finish line and know the directions along the way, pacing myself at the beginning of the race can feel tedious. I suspect the same is probably true for many people. To me, the Christian life is not a sprint but a marathon. How could you run this race carrying a load of bricks and expect to win? Extra weight can bog us down in many areas of life. Debt, unexpected bills, extra work, emotional stress, and just the uncertainty of the unknown can weigh us down and create unnecessary baggage. But, remember, Hebrews 12:1 tells us to *"run with endurance the race that is set before us."* And, in Philippians 3:14, Paul instructs us to *"press toward the goal for the prize of the upward call of God in Christ Jesus."* Some translations refer to this pressing forward as the *"heavenly call"* (CSB) or *"high calling"* (KJV) of God. But I like the wording of the *New King James Version:* the *"upward call."*

> WHEN WE LISTEN TO THE RIGHT VOICES AND MAKE THE RIGHT CHOICES TO MOVE FORWARD, THERE'S NOT ONLY A REWARD, BUT THERE'S AN UPLIFTING.

In this way, when I think of resilience, I think of pressing forward. I believe when we move forward and do all God has for us to do, while making a conscious decision to leave excess baggage behind as God directs, it lightens the load and lifts us up. We can move forward toward the prize and receive the reward God has for us. Hebrews 11:6 says God is *"a rewarder of those who diligently seek Him."* This tells me there's a reward at the end of all the work—at the end of continually moving forward (pressing on) and finishing the journey.

We can think of this in terms of *voices* and *choices*. I believe that when we listen to the right voices and make the right choices to move forward, there's not only a reward, but there's an uplifting.

CHEERING YOU ON

In *The Message*, Philippians 3:13–16 reads:

> *Friends, don't get me wrong: By no means do I count myself an expert in all of this, but I've got my eye on the goal, where God is beckoning us onward—to Jesus. I'm off and running, and I'm not turning back. So let's keep focused on that goal, those of us who want everything God has for us. If any of you have something else in mind, something less than total commitment, God will clear your blurred vision—you'll see it yet! Now that we're on the right track, let's stay on it.*

This is my favorite translation of these verses, and there's something about it that makes me feel like the words themselves are cheering me on, that God is cheering me on. I have a precious friend in ministry named Terri Savelle Foy. She is, without a doubt, one of the most encouraging human beings I've ever known. Her purpose is to lift people up, encourage people to set and reach goals, and always remind people that she is cheering them on. Just as Terri calls herself the "cheerleader of dreams," Philippians 3:13–16 serves as the source of my own encouragement and support. My prayer is that this Scripture cheers you on, too, as you realize that, regardless of what is in the past, it's just that—the past. When you let it go as God directs, the path ahead can be uplifting, rewarding, and just plain amazing.

THE SAND IN THE HOURGLASS

I have a beautiful hourglass that Evelyn, my mother-in-law, gave me. As the sand sifts through it, nothing I can do will speed it up or slow it down. Time is time, and that's that. If we look at the sand in the hourglass as life in general, we realize that what's on top has to happen in its own time, and what's on the bottom has already happened, and we can't do anything about it. We can't change it. And a crucial part of the hourglass is the center tube (neck) through which the sand passes from top to bottom. It represents the present time in our lives. We can choose to get stuck in the bottom of the hourglass, resting in the past. Or we can be motivated by purpose—living in the top of the hourglass, the new thing, propelled forward by God's direction for our life. I want you to see that the excitement of your life isn't in the sand at the bottom of the glass; it's in what is coming. Remember, Philippians 3:14 says, *"Press toward the goal for the prize of the upward call of God in Christ Jesus."* We are in the now. Rather than spending your now focusing on your past, I encourage you to invest in your now by focusing on the future.

NOW IS THE TIME

Oral used to say, "Now is the time. The time is now. God wants to be in the *now* of your life." I have a friend from South Africa who said that the word *now* means something completely different in her country than it means in the United States. People there refer to time as "just now," "now," and "now-now." To her, *now-now* means right now, immediately.

When Jesus was teaching in one of the synagogues centuries ago, He saw a woman who had been bent over, unable to straighten herself up for eighteen long years (Luke 13:10–11). But look what happens in verses 12–13: *"When Jesus saw her, he called her forward and said to her, 'Woman, you are set free ['thou art loosed' KJV] from your infirmity.' Then he put his hands on her, and immediately she straightened up and praised God"* (NIV). What a powerful story!

I believe *now-now* is the time for you to decide to release the past, let go of the excess baggage keeping you from God's highest and best, and be set free. With God's help, you can bounce back from anything that has ever held you back, and you can live a life of joy, peace, fulfilled purpose, and strength.

SUMMARY

1. As I pay close attention to the characteristics of strong godly women, I observe a key quality—resilience. Resilience is the ability to bounce back after a setback. Like freeing a car stuck in the snow, lightening our load and getting unstuck can be freeing when it's done according to God's will and His timing. Read Isaiah 43:18–19 and meditate on what you believe is God's new thing and perfect timing for your particular situation, dream, or vision.

2. Hebrews 12:1–3 refers to the Christian life as a race you need to run with endurance as Jesus did, not losing heart. To win this race, I believe it's important to look ahead, toward the finish line, and to keep going. When you move forward to do all God has for you, while leaving your excess baggage behind as He directs, it can lighten the load and lift you up. You can move toward *"the prize of the upward call of God in Christ Jesus"* (Philippians 3:14).

3. The present time in your life is like the center tube (neck) of an hourglass. We are living in the now. Rather than

spending your now focusing on your past, invest your now focusing on the future.

NOTES TO SELF

Now that you've read this chapter, what notes would you like to write to yourself to help you remember the strength-building points that are most helpful to you or that apply to a specific situation in your life?

_____

_____

_____

_____

_____

I BELIEVE THE BIBLE
TEACHES US IN JAMES 4:8
THAT WE OUGHT TO PRAY NOT
ONLY AS A MEANS OF MAKING
OUR REQUESTS KNOWN TO
GOD, BUT ALSO AS A WAY TO
SPEND TIME WITH HIM.

15

STRONG WOMEN PRAY

The possibilities of prayer run parallel with
the promises of God.
—E. M. Bounds[1]

A friend of ours was enrolled in a doctoral program at Oklahoma State University. Students normally take courses for three-and-a-half to four years and then sit for their comprehensive exam. This exam is academically rigorous, and students may not begin the final phase of the doctoral program, the writing of the doctoral dissertation, until they pass it.

When a student begins a doctoral program, they are assigned to a faculty committee of three or four members. This committee determines the specific classes the student will take and also writes the comprehensive exam that will be given at the end. Just imagine studying for an exam that covers up to four years of courses! Our friend began organizing class material and studying for the exam about ten months in advance.

Finally, the time came for the exam, and he sat for twelve hours of testing over the course of two days. The first day went fine, but on the second day, in the last section of the exam, he ran into a problem. In this research section, the faculty provided six questions and required that three of the six be answered. Our friend answered two with no problem. But as he sat and stared at the remaining four questions, he began to panic because he could not figure out how to answer any one of them. He had been taking classes for three-and-a-half years. He had been preparing for the exam for ten months. He had already been writing this exam for ten hours. And he could not think of how to answer the very last question.

WHAT WOULD YOU DO?

Now, let's stop right here and think about this situation. Maybe you haven't tried to complete an exam to earn your doctorate, but I can imagine you have experienced circumstances that had you feeling the way our friend did. What will you do when you don't know what to do—when your back is metaphorically against the wall and it looks like you are going to fail? I believe the answer is to turn to God in prayer.

Instead of continuing to panic, our friend began to pray and ask God for creative ideas and insight, something he had heard Richard and me encourage people to do for years. He began praying under his breath, "God, I have faithfully taken classes for three-and-a-half years and have diligently studied for this exam. I have put in hours and hours of preparation. God, from everything that I have studied, I'm asking You to help me figure out how I can answer this very last question. Amen." Directly after he said, "Amen," he remembered a case study that had been discussed earlier that semester in a qualitative research class, a study that provided a perfect outline for the answer to the last question on the exam. For the next hour and a half, he wrote his final answer. Later, one of the faculty members said he wanted to commend my friend for how he had answered that particular question. And my friend ended up winning the outstanding student award for his entire class. How did he get there? Hard work, dedication, and diligence, for sure. But he said it was his prayer that got him across the finish line.

> WHAT WILL YOU DO WHEN YOU DON'T
> KNOW WHAT TO DO—WHEN YOUR BACK IS
> METAPHORICALLY AGAINST THE WALL AND IT
> LOOKS LIKE YOU ARE GOING TO FAIL? I BELIEVE
> THE ANSWER IS TO TURN TO GOD IN PRAYER.

THE BOOMERANG PRAYER

SOWING AND REAPING

James 5:16 says, *"Pray one for another, that you may be healed."* For some time, I read this Scripture incorrectly. It does *not* say "that *they* may be healed." It *does* say *"that you may be healed."* I call this a "boomerang prayer" because, as we send it out, it comes back to us in like manner.

Galatians 6:7–9 teaches us that whatever we sow, we will reap. What we sow into other people's lives, we can expect in return. When my grandmother was well past retirement age, I would call her, and she would tell me where she was going that day. In her humorous way, she would say, "I'm headed to the retirement home to pray for the 'older folks.'" Many of those precious "older folks" were younger than she was! But she felt led to do something, to give something to someone else.

TYPE, VIRGINIA, TYPE

One my favorite healing stories is about a lady I worked with for many years. Her name was Virginia, and, without a doubt, she could type faster than anyone I've ever known. If there was a need for something to be typed with tremendous speed and accuracy, Virginia was everyone's go-to person.

One day, Virginia was diagnosed with cancer. This was such a devastating blow to our entire office, as we all loved her so much. She was in need of treatment that would be physically draining, and I wrongly assumed I'd need to look for someone to fill in for a short time. When I walked into the office and heard the sound of Mach-speed typing, I wondered what was going on. There was Virginia, typing and laughing and agreeing "Yes, Lord" to whatever faith-filled message she was typing. When I asked her what she was doing, she said, "I'm typing!" Great answer, but why? She said she was typing her own healing.

Virginia was giving to others in the midst of her need, and she chose to continue her work as a seed sowed to God. In return, she said she was being so filled with the Word and encouragement that she had to continue doing it. Wow! In addition, she took breaks from time to time, saying, "Gotta go." At first, I thought she took these breaks to receive more treatment. But then Virginia told me, "I need to go pray for other cancer patients." She would call, visit, and encourage others, and, as you might guess, those prayers came right back to her for healing. Her attitude, her faith, her giving, and her prayers all contributed to her healing. Eventually, at a very "seasoned" age, Virginia went home to be with the Lord, and I'm certain she fully reaped her reward as one of God's dear and faithful ladies.

FINDING JESUS ON YOUR KNEES

I believe one of the greatest lessons I ever learned about prayer was from what might be one of the greatest lessons Oral ever learned about prayer. He told me this lesson came at the expense of his knees. While Oral was going to school and trying to support his young family, the Lord instructed him to read completely through the four Gospels and the book of Acts three times consecutively and to do it on his knees, in a posture of prayer, within a period of six weeks. Oral believed that if he would do this, he would understand Jesus's love and power in a whole new way. Imagine the discipline it took to do this!

After Oral completed this process, just as the Lord promised, Jesus became even more real to him in a most powerful way. By seeing who Jesus really was to him, he then knew who *he* was. This experience shaped his entire life and ministry. Oral said that from that day on, he began to know and love the ministry of Jesus and the importance of prayer. Throughout his life, Oral said he would find himself chatting with Jesus while on his knees and found that to be his favorite way to pray.

SHOWDOWN WITH THE ENEMY

During the entire time I was pregnant with my daughter Jordan, I had been waiting, expecting, believing, and having such a wonderful time. However, just as I was about to give birth, the spirit of fear came over me. I don't mean I was a little bit afraid. Fear tried to consume me. I called Richard to come help me. As he started to pray, he realized that something was wrong. We started talking about fear and what I was feeling. Normally, Richard would be the first one to jump in and pray. But the Holy Spirit directed him in a different way this time. For some reason, he felt led to tell me I needed to be the one to pray for myself and to put down this fear once and for all.

I knew he was right. Many times, when I needed prayer, I would call Richard. Many times, I would call his dad. And as much as I wanted him to pray for me in that moment of fear, I knew I had to face it by myself. Richard and I both knew it. I went into our bedroom and shut the door. I told the devil this was the showdown. I have no idea why I called it that; all I know is that I was fed up with the devil for pushing me around with fear just as I was preparing to give birth. I commanded him to flee, saying, "Get behind me, Satan!" and told him he would not prevail. Within a matter of minutes, I felt peace, and the fear subsided.

The best thing I can say about the situation is that it was dealt with. In Matthew 16:23, Jesus says, *"Get behind Me, Satan!"* This was behind me. Days later, I went into the hospital, had my beautiful Jordan, brought her home, and understood that the showdown was real. I had to exercise our God-given authority over the devil. While I love to pray for other people, and I love to have other people pray for me, this was one particular time when I knew I had to pray for myself. Something rose up inside of me, and I knew at that moment who I was in Christ, and who Satan was not.

> PRAYER IS FELLOWSHIP (MEANING PERSONAL RELATIONSHIP OR COMPANIONSHIP) WITH GOD.

PRAY AND DON'T GIVE UP

Sometimes, we pray for a situation, and it is resolved seemingly right away; other times, we need to persevere in prayer—either way, pray and persevere in your prayer! Don't give up.

When Jordan was about three, I placed her in her car seat in the back of my car. But because she had unusually long legs, when I pushed the front seat back, her foot became pinched between the seats. She let out a scream, and when I realized what I'd done, I immediately released her foot.

She said, "Pray, Momma, pray!" So, I prayed. A couple of minutes later, she again said, "Pray, Momma, pray!" So, I prayed again. Then, once more, she said, "Pray, Momma, pray!" To which I replied, "Of course." Then I asked, "How many times do you think we should pray, sweetie?" I'll never forget her profound answer. She said, "Pray until the pain stops." What wisdom we can learn from a three-year-old!

Luke 18:1 says, *"Then Jesus told his disciples a parable to show them that they should always pray and not give up"* (NIV). Jesus then told them a story about a persistent widow who kept coming to a judge to ask for justice against her adversary. When I read this Scripture, two things come to my mind about prayer. The first is that prayer is a communication system with words between God and people. The second is that it's not only about words but about being present in a situation. In this parable, the widow *"kept coming to* [the judge]*"* (Luke 18:3 NIV).

When Luke 18:1 says we ought to pray and not give up, it means to not grow weary or become exhausted.[2] The same Greek word translated as "give up" in Luke 18:1 is found in Galatians 6:9, where it says, *"Let us not become weary in doing good, for at the proper time we will reap a harvest if we do not give up"* (NIV). These two Scriptures communicate the same message about not giving up. Ephesians 6:10 says we are to *"be strong in the Lord and in the power of His might."* So I believe that as we spend time in prayer, our tiredness can turn to strength and our supplications can lead to answers. Cultivating a life of prayer and being in God's presence are essential to discovering our true strength.

James 4:8 says, *"Draw near to God and He will draw near to you."* First Chronicles 16:11 says, *"Seek the LORD and his strength; seek his presence continually!"* (ESV). Prayer is fellowship (meaning personal relationship or companionship) with God.

When I need a companion, and I know Richard is around, it strengthens me. When I'm around my family, it strengthens me. When I pray, there are times when certain words are important for me to speak, knowing that God is listening. And I believe there are times when God enjoys speaking to me when He knows I am listening. That, to me, is fellowship and companionship with God. We keep one another company. Many times, Richard and I can be in a room and talk and talk and talk. Other times, we can be in the same room and say nothing, yet we still enjoy companionship and keeping one another company. I believe the Bible teaches us in James 4:8 that we ought to pray not only as a means of making our requests known to God, but also as a way to spend time with Him. I can't encourage you strongly enough to spend time in prayer—time being with God as a companion.

SUMMARY

1. James 5:16 says, *"Pray one for another, that you may be healed."* Note the word *"you."* This isn't just for someone else; it's about your own healing too. This is a "boomerang prayer," one that comes back to you when you pray it for others. According to Galatians 6:7–9, you reap what you sow. If you sow the goodness of God, isn't that what you can expect in return? Whatever you are believing God for in your life, consider doing something to sow that very thing into the lives of others.

2. Luke 18:1 says to *"always pray and not give up"* (NIV). You can see from this Scripture the importance of being persistent in asking God for what you are believing for until you receive His answer. But there's another aspect to prayer that I believe is also as important as petition, and that's presence. First Chronicles 16:11 says, *"Seek the Lord and his strength; seek his presence continually!"* (ESV). Just as we find comfort and strength when we spend time with certain people, we can find comfort and

strength in God's presence. The more time you spend with Him, the more you can expect that when you "*draw near to God...He will draw near to you*" (James 4:8).

NOTES TO SELF

Now that you've read this chapter, what notes would you like to write to yourself to help you remember the strength-building points that are most helpful to you or that apply to a specific situation in your life?

_____

_____

_____

_____

_____

I BELIEVE GIVERS INCREASE
IN SOME WAY EVERY TIME
THEY GIVE.

16

STRONG WOMEN GIVE

For it is in giving that we receive.
—St. Francis of Assisi

When you think of women you consider strong, how many of them are generous? Probably, a lot of them. I believe giving is a characteristic of strong godly women. I have found they give of their time, their knowledge, their experience, their leadership, their influence and example, their encouragement, and their correction when needed (in appropriate ways). They give of their financial resources as God leads them. The overall form in which they give is not what's most important. What matters most is that they have generous hearts, and they look for ways and places to give. They seek to bless others, and, in turn, they are blessed. I believe this is one of the most important keys to their strength. I believe givers increase in some way every time they give.

The apostle Paul wrote in Acts 20:35, *"And remember the words of the Lord Jesus, that He said, 'It is more blessed to give than to receive.'"* I think Paul's point in reminding the people of the early church about this teaching of Jesus was to highlight the productivity of giving. What's really interesting to me is that the Greek word translated as *"blessed"* is sometimes presented as the word "happy."

Second Corinthians 9:7 says that *"God loves a cheerful giver."* I believe giving actually makes us cheerful and happy. And I wonder, could it be that people are cheerful as they give because of Scriptures such as Luke 6:38? In this verse, Jesus says, *"Give, and it will be given to you: good measure, pressed down, shaken together, and running over will be put into your bosom. For with the same measure that you use, it will be measured back to you."* Could it be because of Scriptures such as Galatians 6:7? The apostle Paul wrote in this verse, *"Do not be deceived: God is not mocked, for whatever one sows, that will he also reap"* (ESV). Or could the fact that we are happy when we give simply mean that we were created with a heart to give, just as our Creator God and His Son, Jesus, have generous, giving hearts? Since we are created in God's image, is giving embedded in the fiber of our souls from birth, and we just have to figure out what to do with it in order to please Him?

Answer: probably a combination of all of the above.

If God wants us to be givers, He must have created the environment and resources that enable us to have something to give. Many people think they don't have anything to give. But I believe that's because, generally speaking, when people think of giving, they think of giving resources of money or material things. While this type of giving is important, and it's lovely to be generous with things, I also believe that we are supernaturally infused with an amazing nature to give in other ways. Our job is to discover what our gifts are and to realize that we do have *something* we can give.

In Matthew 7:7, Jesus says, *"Ask, and it will be given to you; seek, and you will find; knock, and it will be opened to you."* I believe this Scripture can come alive for us if we truly ask, seek, and knock. Daniel 2:22 says that God *"reveals deep and hidden things; he knows what lies in darkness"* (NIV). Consider asking God to show you what you can give that you might not even be aware of. If God reveals it, are you willing to give it? There are times when it's very easy for me to say yes, and other times when it's actually more difficult. Jesus says, *"Freely you have received, freely give"* (Matthew 10:8). And while I realize Jesus was talking about praying for the sick, the concept of giving to others is still relatively the same. As God blesses you, He can make you a blessing to others. As the old saying teaches us, "What goes around comes around."

> IF GOD WANTS US TO BE GIVERS, HE MUST HAVE
> CREATED THE ENVIRONMENT AND RESOURCES
> THAT ENABLE US TO HAVE SOMETHING TO GIVE.

PAYING IT FORWARD

Even in our fallen world, where retribution and payback are all too common, there is a practice going around called "paying it forward." When someone does something nice for you, instead of paying them back directly, you "pay it forward" to someone else, sometimes even a stranger. For example, one person will pay for someone else's order in a drive-through, and when that person finds out their order has been paid for, they pay for the order of the person behind them. This can go on through a long line of people.

The idea of paying it forward, as I see it, isn't something new; it's something old. I think of Matthew 10:8 again. That is the "pay it forward" concept if ever there were one. It's the quintessential golden rule—treating others in the same manner in which you would like to be treated. Not only is this a wonderful practice for friends, relatives, and sometimes even strangers, but it's something wonderful you can do for yourself.

Let's take a good look at Philippians 4:13: *"I can do all things through Christ who strengthens me."* While I am not asking you to be selfish, I want to point out that the words *I* and *me* are included in this verse. I believe it's all right to see yourself as strong, successful, and capable. We see this principle illustrated clearly when we're on an airplane. When flight attendants instruct passengers concerning safety rules, they tell adults who are seated next to children to put their own masks on first and then assist the children. The premise behind this is that those who are operating from a position of strength can help those who are not as strong. As you become strong in your thinking and believing, as well as in other areas, you can become a positive force to help those in need. You can become a giver.

Giving requires having something to give. Whether you give your time, your talent, your finances, your smile, a good attitude, or anything else, it starts with believing you have something to give to others. Allowing Satan to sell you short regarding yourself can stop your cycle of giving to someone else. However, when you acknowledge and receive all that God has given you, then, as you prosper, you can have something to pass on to the next person. For instance, as you prosper in your thinking, you can pass good thoughts on to someone else. In whatever way you prosper, you can pay it forward, creating a cycle of God's blessing.

The key to giving is to start *somewhere*. Marathon runners must decide to take the first steps before they can run the full twenty-six-plus miles. Zechariah 4:10 says, *"Do not despise these small beginnings, for the LORD rejoices to see the work begin"* (NLT). When you give something to God, it can be multiplied. Remember that Jesus fed five thousand people with five loaves of bread and two fish. But the little boy who brought them had to agree to start the process by giving what he had.

BE A CHILD OF GOD AND CHANGE THE WORLD

As children of God, we are members of His family. Galatians 4:6 says that God is our Abba Father, a term indicating intimacy and obedience. In addition, Paul says in Romans 8:17 that we are part of God's family and joint heirs with Jesus. We not only have family privileges, but we are expected to act like family. This is where the word *child* can be used as an acronym:

Choose

Humble

Increase

Love

Disciple

We can *choose* to be *humble* as we *increase* in all the good things of God. We can *love* one another and be Jesus's *disciples*, His voice to our generation.

We can be a direct reflection of the life that Jesus lived, and we can give out of the gifts we have received. We can pass on what we have to others for the next generation.

There is a saying that has been attributed to an unknown monk from AD 1100 that goes like this:

When I was a young man, I wanted to change the world. I found it was difficult to change the world, so I tried to change my nation. When I found I couldn't change the nation, I began to focus on my town. I couldn't change the town, and as an older man, I tried to change my family. Now, as an old man, I realize the only thing I can change is myself, and suddenly I realize that if long ago I had changed myself, I could have made an impact on my family. My family and I could have made an impact on our town. Their impact could have changed the nation and I could indeed have changed the world.[1]

> THE NEXT TIME SATAN TRIES TO CONVINCE YOU
> THAT YOU HAVE NOTHING TO GIVE, YOU COULD
> REMIND HIM THAT *HE* HAS NOTHING TO GIVE,
> BUT *YOU* HAVE EVERYTHING TO GIVE BECAUSE
> JESUS GAVE EVERYTHING FOR YOU.

Perhaps you might read the previous paragraph again. There is so much potential locked up inside of us, and God has placed it there. Satan's job is to make certain we don't see it or use it. Our job is to make certain we do. I believe you can reach your potential by overcoming your fears and failures through a close personal relationship with God. This doesn't mean you avoid them, because no one is perfect. The only perfect person who walked the earth was Jesus, and He does not expect our perfection, just our willingness and obedience. Isaiah 1:19 says that if we are *"willing and obedient,"* we will *"eat the good of the land."* This is what God requires, and it's also what He rewards.

I want you to begin to realize that God is your refuge and your fortress (Psalm 91:2). Once you understand this in your own life, you can point someone else to this truth in God's Word. God is our *"very present help in trouble"* (Psalm 46:1). As you were helped, you can direct someone else to be helped in the way in which God helped you.

So the next time Satan tries to convince you that you have nothing to give, you could remind him that *he* has nothing to give, but *you* have everything to give because Jesus gave everything for you.

GIVING SOMETHING AWAY LEAVES YOU WITH MORE, NOT LESS

Malachi 3:10–12 says:

> *"Bring all the tithes into the storehouse, that there may be food in My house, and try Me now in this," says the LORD of hosts,*

"if I will not open for you the windows of heaven and pour out for you such blessing that there will not be room enough to receive it. And I will rebuke the devourer for your sakes, so that he will not destroy the fruit of your ground, nor shall the vine fail to bear fruit for you in the field," says the LORD of hosts; "and all nations will call you blessed, for you will be a delightful land," says the LORD of hosts.

Here's an interesting question: When was the last time nations called you "blessed"? Of course, God was talking about the nation of Israel here. This was a message to the Old Testament priests who had stopped putting God first, neglecting to give Him a tithe of their grain, wine, and oil. A tithe is a tenth off the top of someone's income or resources. This may sound like a lot, but in the next verse, the Lord says He will pour out such a blessing on them that they won't even have room for it.

So how can you give 10 percent and still increase? Doesn't it seem like you would be decreasing if you gave something away? Many times, I talk about the principles of God's kingdom being the opposite of those of the kingdom of the world. In God's kingdom, to receive, we give. In the natural realm, this doesn't make sense. But Malachi is very clear that when people honor God with their tithes, they will be blessed and increase, not decrease.

To further confirm what He is saying, the Lord tells His people to *"try Me,"* which means to let God prove He will do what He promises. Now, we know from Deuteronomy 6:16 that God tells us not to put Him to the test, and Jesus also quotes this verse in Matthew 4:7 and Luke 4:12. (*"Test"* is used in various Bible translations, while the *New King James Version* uses the word *"tempt."*) But in Malachi, God is actually telling the priests to test Him. According to *Strong's Concordance*, the Hebrew word for "try" or "test" is the equivalent of "put me on trial."[2] Think about why God says to put Him on trial and see if He doesn't do all He says He will.

God felt so strongly about the priests not paying their tithes, He considered them to be thieves, robbing Him of what was rightfully His (Malachi 3:8–9). Now, I didn't make that statement—God did—and I have to believe He put it into His Word for a reason. And while it's true that this incident occurred during Old Testament times, there are several Scriptures in both the Old and New Testaments that validate the principle that you will be blessed when you give. In Genesis, Abraham gave a tithe of the goods he recovered in the battle against the four kings (Genesis 14:18–20). Immediately afterward, he became the most blessed person on earth.

I believe there's a direct correlation between giving and being blessed, and Malachi confirms it. We are no longer under the Old Testament law. However, the principle of giving (in our case, voluntarily, out of love and obedience to God) is still valid for Christians (Luke 6:38). As believers, we have received the greatest gift of all—salvation through faith in Jesus. I believe we should be the most generous givers on earth. After all, we saw earlier that God loves a generous giver (2 Corinthians 9:7). I believe that when you bring your offering into God's storehouse and "test Him in this," He will open the windows of heaven and pour out a blessing where there isn't even enough room to contain it all.

Oral used to say that in the Old Testament, you paid your tithe under the law, but in the New Testament, it's not "a debt you owe but a seed you sow." While I can't tell you what to give, where to give, how to give, or who to give to, I can say that I make my decisions to give with a heart that desires to give to God based on the verse I mentioned earlier—Luke 6:38 in the New Testament. When it says, *"Give, and it will be given to you,"* I think one of the most important words is *"it."* What is the *"it"* that you are giving? Is it your love, your time, your encouragement, your talents or abilities, your wisdom, or your finances? And is "it" being given back to you? The simple, two-letter word *it* becomes very important based on this Scripture.

Galatians 6:9 says, *"And let us not grow weary of doing good, for in due season we will reap, if we do not give up"* (ESV). Galatians 6:7 says, *"Do not be deceived, God is not mocked; for whatever a man sows, that he will also reap."* I believe that in light of this, giving is a very important responsibility.

But why is it so important? Does God need our money? I don't believe He does—at least not for Himself. The Bible says in Revelation 21:18–20 that the new Jerusalem has streets of gold. The walls are made out of jasper, and the gates are made out of pearl. There is no lack whatsoever. I believe it comes back again to what Oral said: "It's not a debt you owe but a seed you sow." Instead of looking at tithing from the perspective that God is trying to take something from us, I look at it from the viewpoint that God is trying to get something *to* us. The Bible says that when we are givers, we are to become receivers. When we sow, we are to reap. So without giving, how can there be receiving?

I find it interesting that when someone from the world prospers—lives in abundance—they don't seem to be criticized by others in the world, even if they obtained that abundance in perhaps ungodly ways. But, in my observation, when someone in the kingdom begins to receive, immediately red flags go up and questions are asked—even among some other Christians. I always try to gauge my decisions in that area according to Psalm 1:1–3, which says, *"Blessed is the one who does not walk in step with the wicked or stand in the way that sinners take or sit in the company of mockers, but whose delight is in the law of the LORD, and who meditates on his law day and night.... Whatever they do prospers"* (NIV).

The Bible makes reference to giving what we can give, whether it's through tangible resources or intangible ones. Again, when we give, we receive. When we sow, we reap. By listening to the world's advice about the kingdom of God, we can get into a mess. But I believe that when we base our decisions on Scriptures like Psalm 1:1–3, we prosper. For me, listening to the world's advice on the Bible from those who don't know its teachings is like going to Goliath for advice on David's ministry. Goliath doesn't see it from the same perspective. I don't want to go to the world for advice on what God says about His kingdom. I'm satisfied to just trust the Word of God—to believe it and obey what God says. I believe that when I sow, I reap, no matter what the world says. I'd rather obey God and deal with the persecution of the world than listen to the world and be disobedient to God. God's Word wins out for me every time. There is no question in my mind that the greatest gift that's ever been given to the world is the gift of everlasting life through Jesus Christ. If Jesus can give His life for me, I can give generously in obedience to God's Word.

SUMMARY

1. I believe giving is a characteristic of strong godly women. And as they seek to bless others, in turn, God says He will bless them. The Greek word translated as *"blessed"* in Acts 20:35 in many Bible versions is sometimes presented as "happy." Second Corinthians 9:7 says that *"God loves a cheerful giver."* I believe giving actually makes us cheerful, and it's in our nature as Christians to want to give. Ask God to show you what and where you can give, and as you do, I believe that you can experience His joy.

2. The practice of "paying it forward" is expressed in Matthew 10:8: *"Freely you have received, freely give."* But have you ever thought of this as being something you do for yourself? I believe it's all right to see yourself as

strong, successful, and capable. Giving requires having something to give. Don't allow Satan to sell you short regarding yourself. Remember, as you prosper, you have something to pass on to the next person.

3. I like to use an acronym to express what it means to be God's child: the acronym CHILD indicates we can *choose* to be *humble* as we *increase* in all the good things of God, and we can *love* one another and be Jesus's *disciples*—His voice to our generation. I want you to believe that there is so much potential locked up inside of you. So the next time Satan tries to convince you that you have nothing to give, you could remind him that *he* has nothing to give, but *you* have everything to give because Jesus gave everything for you.

4. In God's kingdom, to receive, we give. I believe there's a direct correlation between giving and being blessed, and Malachi 3:10–11 validates this. Rather than seeing tithing as just an Old Testament law, I like to give out of a heart of love and obedience as God directs. I also give in response to having received the greatest gift of all—salvation through faith in Jesus. When you bring your offering into God's storehouse and "test Him in this," I believe He will open the windows of heaven and pour out a blessing where there isn't even enough room to contain it all.

NOTES TO SELF

Now that you've read this chapter, what notes would you like to write to yourself to help you remember the strength-building points that are most helpful to you or that apply to a specific situation in your life?

_____

_____

_____

_____

_____

17

STRONG WOMEN CHOOSE FAITH OVER FEAR

Faith does not eliminate questions.
But faith knows where to take them.
—Elisabeth Elliot[1]

As believers, we hear the word *faith* often. Perhaps you are familiar with the portion of Romans 1:17 that says, *"The just shall live by faith,"* or with 2 Corinthians 5:7, which says, *"We walk by faith, not by sight."*

Faith has been defined as:

1. complete trust or confidence in someone or something

2. strong belief in God or in the doctrines of a religion, based on spiritual apprehension rather than proof[2]

I particularly like the way the *Amplified Bible, Classic Edition* describes faith in Colossians 1:4: *"For we have heard of your faith in Christ Jesus [the leaning of your entire human personality on Him in absolute trust and confidence in His power, wisdom, and goodness]."* Let this thought sink in for a moment. According to this verse, to live by faith is to lean your entire human personality on Jesus with absolute trust and confidence in His power, wisdom, and goodness. I believe this is exactly how strong godly women are created to live.

FAITH TRIUMPHS OVER FEAR

If someone were to ask a group of Christians which of Jesus's disciples was the strongest, I would think many people would say, "Peter." In the Gospels, the book of Acts, and the letters that bear his name, Peter certainly comes across as brave and bold, with a strong personality.

One of the Bible stories that has fascinated me from the first time I read it is the story of Peter walking on water. We read in Matthew 14 that, after Jesus's cousin John the Baptist was beheaded at King Herod's command, Jesus climbed into a boat so He could spend some time alone. When He returned to land, a large crowd gathered around Him, and they were hungry. Jesus instructed His disciples to feed them using only five loaves of bread and two fish. He worked a miracle, and five thousand men, plus women and children, had enough to eat (verses 1–21).

After this, the disciples got into a boat to cross to the other side of the Sea of Galilee, and they encountered a storm. Jesus had stayed behind to dismiss the crowd, then went to pray on a mountainside. When He was ready to join His disciples just before dawn the next morning, He chose the most efficient mode of transportation (for Him, not us!)—walking on water. When He arrived at the boat that was carrying the disciples across the water, they looked up, saw Him, and immediately began to panic (verses 22–26). The *New International Version* says that *"they were terrified"* (Matthew 14:26). Keep this thought in mind as you consider what transpired next.

The disciples saw Jesus walking toward them and thought they were seeing a ghost. Fear overtook them. But then Jesus spoke, saying, *"Take courage!"* (verse 27 NIV). Jesus told them to take courage rather than take fear. Isn't it amazing that, in difficult situations, we can choose what to "take"? We can take fear, or we can take courage. I like the sound—and the idea—of taking courage so much better than the notion of being afraid.

Jesus immediately identified Himself, saying, *"It is I. Don't be afraid"* (verse 27 NIV). Then Peter made an amazing comment: *"Lord, if it's you,...tell me to come to you on the water"* (verse 28 NIV). This was someone so afraid of what he thought was a ghost that the Bible says he was terrified, along with the other disciples. Then, when Jesus identified Himself, instead of being excited or relieved that He wasn't a ghost, Peter wanted proof. I can understand wanting proof. But instead of saying, "Jesus, show us a miracle," or "Jesus, show us some kind of evidence," Peter basically said, "Lord, if it's really You, let me walk on water." At first, Peter was terrified of a ghost. Then he wanted to walk on water. None of this makes any rational sense. However, throughout the New Testament, we read about times when Peter didn't seem to make sense (see, for example, Matthew 26:69–75; Mark 14:66–72; Luke 22:55–62; John 18:16–18, 25–27; Galatians 2:11–14), so this statement seems to be consistent with his nature.

> JESUS TOLD THEM TO TAKE COURAGE RATHER
> THAN TAKE FEAR. ISN'T IT AMAZING THAT, IN
> DIFFICULT SITUATIONS, WE CAN CHOOSE WHAT
> TO "TAKE"?

Jesus told Peter to come out and walk on the water. And Peter literally walked on water. A man—*a human being*—*walked on water*. In no way do I recommend this to anyone, but since it's in the Bible, let's see what Jesus thought about it and what we can learn from it. The Bible goes on to say that the storm began to blow, and Peter panicked again. As fear set in, Peter stopped focusing on Jesus and started to focus on the storm. The moment he took his eyes off Jesus, he began to sink. His comment was, *"Lord, save me!"* (Matthew 14:30). Immediately, Jesus reached out to catch him (verse 31).

Peter's wishy-washy, back-and-forth personality was so evident in this scene. One minute, he thought he saw a ghost and was afraid. The next minute, he was full of faith and wanted to walk on water. The next minute, he saw a storm and panicked again. Finally, Jesus saved him. Then Jesus spoke a most wonderful line: *"You of little faith, why did you doubt?"* (verse 31).

Peter heard Jesus call him to walk on water. He also heard Him ask why he had doubted. What we hear is important, but what we *do* with what we hear is also important. If we are surrounded by fear, it's entirely possible that we can become filled with fear—not only in our soul (mind, will, and emotions) but also in our spirit (inmost being). And where fear is, faith seems to dim.

God has given us an opportunity to overrule that fear based on His Word, and that's what strong godly women can do. I believe the opportunity to triumph over fear comes through hearing God's Word, believing it, decreeing it, and walking out what we feel God is telling us. To be a woman of true, God-infused strength, filled with faith, consider doing these four steps, as needed, toward overcoming fear:

1. Hear God's Word.

2. Believe God's Word.

3. Decree (speak aloud in faith) God's Word.

4. Walk out the truth of God's Word.

HEARING THE WORD BUILDS OUR FAITH

Romans 10:17 says, *"So then faith comes by hearing, and hearing by the word of God."* The more we put God's Word into our hearts and minds, the more that Word builds our faith—until faith begins to overflow in our lives and becomes our first response to situations. Psalm 119:105 says God's Word is *"a lamp to my feet and a light to my path."* So if I'm in the dark concerning something, the easiest thing for me to do is to open the Word and let it shine light on the situation I'm facing. According to Hebrews 4:12, God's Word is *"living and powerful, and sharper than any two-edged sword."* This means that it can metaphorically make an opening in our lives for good to come in and for bad to be removed.

> AS WE BIND OURSELVES TO GOD'S WORDS AND PUT OUR HEARTS AND MINDS INTO AGREEMENT WITH THEM, WE CAN RECEIVE THE PROMISES ATTACHED TO THEM.

Do you remember the old saying "Sticks and stones may break my bones, but words will never hurt me"? As lighthearted as this adage sounds, I believe it's as far from biblical truth as it can be.

I have come to believe we don't simply *say* our words, we *spray* our words. When words leave our lips, they are infused into the atmosphere. It's like spraying perfume. The minute the mist comes out of the bottle, the aroma, like our words, affects and permeates the atmosphere, and it can linger all day.

In Matthew 18:18–19, Jesus says, *"Whatever you bind on earth will be bound in heaven, and whatever you loose on earth will be loosed in heaven."* So, what are you binding or attaching yourself to with your words? Are you attaching yourself to what God says about your situation and receiving all His promises? Or are you attaching yourself to your problem and all that goes along with it? As we bind ourselves to God's words and put our hearts and minds into agreement with them, we can receive the promises attached to them.

UNSHAKABLE FAITH

What makes athletes great? Is it their natural athletic ability? Is it their strength? Is it their workout regimen? Well, most likely, yes, to all these questions. But I think there's something else that makes an athlete—or any other disciplined person who achieves an element of success—great. It's that they *believe* they can do whatever they need to do. Their belief is evidence of their faith. Said another way, their faith is their belief system in action. I can think of several women of faith, among others, that the Bible mentions who put their beliefs into action:

- Sarah (Hebrews 11:11)

- Deborah (Judges 4:4–9)

- The widow of Zarephath (1 Kings 17)

- The Shunammite woman (2 Kings 4:8–37)

- Mary Magdalene (Matthew 28:1–8; Mark 16:9–11; Luke 24:1–10; John 20:11–18)

All these women lived, acted, and endured by faith.

The interesting thing about people who lived in Bible times, as well as people today, is that they all have so much in common. These women may have lived in different eras from the one we do, but we have all faced similar struggles. A struggle is still a struggle, regardless of when or where it happens. The women in the above list had choices to make during seasons of challenge, just as we do. They chose to operate in excellence.

In addition, Daniel 5:12 says that Daniel had *"an excellent spirit."* Notice that it doesn't say he was perfect or had a perfected spirit. It says he had an *excellent* spirit. I don't believe God is looking for perfection, but I do believe He's looking for excellence. In that excellence, I believe He is looking for us to be committed to the tasks to which He calls us. This doesn't mean we do the tasks perfectly. It simply means we can stretch our faith and make a conscious decision to do all we can do to bring the tasks to fruition in the most excellent way possible.

People in the Bible faced difficult decisions, and people today do too. But I believe no matter who you are or what time period you live in, you will confront many difficult decisions that must be made by faith. When we make decisions based on faith, the outcome can be completely different from when we make decisions based on fear. The women in the Bible whom I mentioned earlier faced problems, but they also had promises—the promises of God. They had to decide to stay strong both as they dealt with their problems *and* as they pursued those promises or waited for them to manifest. Regardless of the problem, they stuck to the promise of God—and this empowered them to fulfill His plan for their lives. Plans may become difficult. People may become difficult. But as we experience something or someone difficult, we can turn to God's promises in His Word and expect those promises to be effective because they are covered with His grace.

Remember, Romans 10:17 says that *"faith comes by hearing, and hearing* [is] *by the word of God."* Because of this, one of the most important things I've ever done to invest in myself is to pour God's Word into my heart. I made a list of Scriptures about faith, and when I feel the need to remind myself of the benefits of faith over fear, I go to my list and see what the Word says.

I want to share my list of faith Scriptures with you so you can also rehearse them whenever you face a unique challenge or find yourself in a battle against fear. James 2:20 says that faith without good deeds, or works (meaning corresponding action), is useless. So as soon as you see words of faith in Scripture, I want you to pause and evaluate them against your choices. In the list below, many of the verses are not printed in their entirety. I have included the portion of the verses that deals directly with faith, but I would encourage you to read the verses in their context. As you build your faith and apply it to your walk with Christ, try to find time in your own studies to examine the full verses and what they mean to you. You may want to do this a little at a time, but I encourage you to get the Word of God into your heart and mind. As you start this practice, stretch out your faith so that, as you hear the Word, you can believe it, decree it, and walk it out.

> *When Jesus heard it, He marveled, and said to those who followed, "Assuredly, I say to you, I have not found such great faith, not even in Israel!"* (Matthew 8:10)

> *Be of good cheer, daughter; your faith has made you well.* (Matthew 9:22)

> *According to your faith let it be done to you.* (Matthew 9:29 NIV)

> *O woman, great is your faith! Let it be to you as you desire.* (Matthew 15:28)

> *If you have faith as small as a mustard seed, you can say to this mountain, "Move from here to there," and it will move. Nothing will be impossible for you.* (Matthew 17:20 NIV)

> *Have faith in God.* (Mark 11:22)

> *And Stephen, full of faith and power, did great wonders and signs among the people.* (Acts 6:8)

Will their unbelief make the faithfulness of God without effect? (Romans 3:3)

Thus also faith by itself, if it does not have works, is dead. (James 2:17)

That your faith should not be in the wisdom of men but in the power of God. (1 Corinthians 2:5)

For we walk by faith, not by sight. (2 Corinthians 5:7)

Examine yourselves as to whether you are in the faith. Test yourselves. (2 Corinthians 13:5)

That we might receive the promise of the Spirit through faith. (Galatians 3:14)

For by grace you have been saved through faith. (Ephesians 2:8)

Hebrews 11 (entire chapter)

Looking unto Jesus, the author and finisher of our faith. (Hebrews 12:2)

THE FAITH HALL OF FAME

Hebrews 11 is often called "The Faith Hall of Fame" because it lists many biblical heroes of our faith. I'd like to mention some of these people and provide references where you can read their stories in the Bible. And, just a thought: take note of the fact that before the description of each person mentioned in Hebrews 11, we see the words *"by faith."* To me, this explains how they were able to do all they were called to do. And because people are basically the same from age to age and place to place, I believe theirs is a good example to follow as you endeavor to do all God calls you to.

+ *"By faith Abel..."* (Hebrews 11:4; see Genesis 4:4)

+ *"By faith Enoch..."* (Hebrews 11:5; see Genesis 5:24)

+ *"By faith Noah..."* (Hebrews 11:7; see Genesis 6:9–22)

+ *"By faith Abraham..."* (Hebrews 11:8, 17; see Genesis 12:1–9)

+ *"By faith Sarah..."* (Hebrews 11:11; see Genesis 21:1–2)

+ *"By faith Isaac..."* (Hebrews 11:20; see Genesis 27:27–40)

+ *"By faith Jacob..."* (Hebrews 11:21; see Genesis 48:1–20)

+ *"By faith Joseph..."* (Hebrews 11:22; see Genesis 50:24–26)

+ *"By faith Moses..."* (Hebrews 11:23, 24; see Exodus 2:2, 11–15; 12:1–14)

+ *"By faith...Rahab..."* (Hebrews 11:31; see Joshua 2:1–21; 6:25)

And, finally, Hebrews 11:32 reads, *"What more shall I say?"* To me, that says it all. Point taken!

SUMMARY

1. In the midst of a storm, Jesus told His disciples to *"take courage!"* (Matthew 14:27 NIV). This is a lesson we can use when facing fear. We can decide what to "take"— fear or courage. Matthew 14 indicates that, to take courage, we are to keep our focus on Jesus.

2. In becoming a woman of true godly strength, filled with faith, consider these four steps to help overcome fear: (1) hear God's Word, (2) believe God's Word, (3) decree (speak aloud in faith) God's Word, and (4) walk out the truth of God's Word. The more of God's Word you put into your heart and mind, the more empowered you can become to face and conquer fear.

3. There are many people of faith in the Bible (see Hebrews 11 for several examples). Like them, I have had to face decisions and put my faith in the promises of God. To help build your faith, you can do what I have done by making a list of faith Scriptures to read and meditate on.

NOTES TO SELF

Now that you've read this chapter, what notes would you like to write to yourself to help you remember the strength-building points that are most helpful to you or that apply to a specific situation in your life?

_____

_____

_____

_____

WHEN I LET MY SPIRIT GIVE
DIRECTION TO MY SOUL,
AND THEN MY SOUL FILTERS
THAT DIRECTION THROUGH
THE WORD OF GOD, I HAVE
A MUCH BETTER CHANCE
OF CARRYING OUT GOD'S
INSTRUCTIONS IN THE WAY
HIS WORD CALLS FOR.

18

STRONG WOMEN GUARD THEIR SOUL

What good will it be for someone to gain the whole world,
yet forfeit their soul? Or what can anyone give in exchange
for their soul?
—Matthew 16:26 (NIV)

The Bible says that we were created as triune, or three-part, beings. We are spirit; we have a soul (comprised of the mind, will, and emotions); and we live in a body. There is a divine order to how we operate our daily lives based on these three components. The spirit is our direct link to God. As believers, we read and receive truth from the Word of God. We process it through our souls, and then we express it and act on it in the flesh, through our bodies.

STRESS LESS

Some people can live their entire lives based on the feelings of the moment. They let their minds run free instead of disciplining them according to God's Word. They use their will to make choices that do not honor God or benefit themselves. And they allow their emotions to manage them instead of learning to manage their emotions in godly ways, a topic that Bible teacher Joyce Meyer has taught for years. I know that, even as a Christian, I've done this, and I have to get myself back on track and guard my emotions and my soul to make sure I'm in harmony with God's Word.

When I operate from my soul, especially my emotions, without a connection to God in my spirit, I can become anxious and fearful. That fear and worry can lead to stress. If I let my soul drive my life, I can move quickly in the wrong direction. But when I let my spirit give direction to my soul, and then my soul filters that direction through the Word of God, I have a much better chance of carrying out God's instructions in the way His Word calls for.

The soul, therefore, plays an important role in my daily life. What I feed my soul, so to speak, can determine the outcome of each decision I make and move me toward success or failure. I believe that just as the human body has a hard time thriving on nothing but junk food, the soul cannot thrive on nothing but junk in our mind, will, and emotions. If I want enough energy to last through the day, it's crucial for me to fuel my physical body with the nutrients it needs to stay strong. The same principle applies to my soul. So, the question is, what are you feeding your soul today? And is it enough to empower your mind, will, and emotions to lead you to success?

SPEAKING FROM THE SOUL

The strong godly women I have observed often speak from their soul, but in order to attain a godly outcome, they have to speak words that align with God's Word instead of whatever else might have just been fed to them. If what they are feeding their soul is contrary to the Word, then their mind, will, and emotions can operate according to the flesh and to their circumstances. For me to succeed God's way, I have to get my instructions from the

Spirit of God. Operating the world's way and not according to the kingdom of God can cause our flesh to carry out the wrong instructions, sending us in the wrong direction. It's like osmosis: we absorb what we hear around us. What I hear from the outside permeates the inside, and I respond accordingly. But when we hear something in the world, we don't have to process it as the world does—we can run it through a "spiritual filter." As believers, we are not to be moved by the world or its ways but by the kingdom of God. If we immediately react to everything we hear in the world, it could lead to devastation. But when we process it through the Word of God, it can result in revelation.

> WHEN WE HEAR SOMETHING IN THE WORLD, WE DON'T HAVE TO PROCESS IT AS THE WORLD DOES—WE CAN RUN IT THROUGH A "SPIRITUAL FILTER." AS BELIEVERS, WE ARE NOT TO BE MOVED BY THE WORLD OR ITS WAYS BUT BY THE KINGDOM OF GOD.

SPIRITUAL INFUSIONS

One way to effectively process what we are receiving into our minds and emotions is to be consciously aware of what I call *spiritual infusions*. One definition of the word *infusion* is "the introduction of a new element or quality into something."[1] An infusion into the physical body can be used to hydrate or nourish us. In the same way, an infusion of the Word of God can hydrate or nourish our souls. We constantly infuse our souls with words and thoughts. What we do with those words and thoughts can alter our lives, depending on how we react or respond to them.

But, again, here's the big question: What are you feeding your soul? Who and what are you attaching yourself to and allowing to influence your soul and to steer the ship of your life? Are you attaching yourself to fear, worry, negativity, and defeat but expecting a positive, godly outcome? Or are you attaching yourself to love, peace, joy, and prosperity and expecting a godly outcome? The next big question, and perhaps the most important one, is, where is that attachment coming from? Is it from a place of godly influence or ungodly influence?

As I go about my daily life, I encounter positive things, negative things, and a host of things in between. But that does not mean that I attach myself to them. If you plant apple seeds, don't be surprised if the harvest is apples. If you attach yourself to the soul of another person, should there be any surprise when you begin to think, choose, or feel like them? If you are going in one direction with the Spirit of the Lord but then attach yourself to a person, circumstance, movie, social media platform, or something else contrary to what you know to be the Word of God, does that create a conflict in the way you think and process through your soul (your mind, will, and emotions)?

THE BENEFITS

Psalm 103:1–5 says:

> Bless the LORD, O my soul; and all that is within me, bless His holy name! Bless the LORD, O my soul, and forget not all His benefits: who forgives all your iniquities, who heals all your diseases, who redeems your life from destruction, who crowns you with lovingkindness and tender mercies, who satisfies your mouth with good things, so that your youth is renewed like the eagle's.

Remember, the soul consists of the mind, the will, and the emotions. It is the seat of our emotions and passion. When we bless the Lord with our soul, benefits will follow. If we don't bless the Lord with our soul, should we receive the benefits? When, as an act of my spirit, I begin to worship God and praise His name, I change the atmosphere from the natural to the supernatural. When I absorb the presence of God through praise and worship, and when I begin to bless the Lord with my mind, will, and emotions, the outcome of my expectations can switch from the natural to the supernatural.

THE GENUINE

Years ago, I heard the term "soul ties" in certain Christian circles. I recall the connotation to have been something like an unhealthy relationship between two people. Today, the term is popular in secular circles and describes any kind of spiritual or emotional bond connecting people in a way that can be either detrimental or helpful. The term now has both positive and negative connotations.

Sometimes, God uses relationships that involve connections between aspects of the soul for His purposes. For example, in Ruth 1:16–17, Ruth made a commitment to stick with her mother-in-law, Naomi, and to follow Naomi's God. This involved her mind, her will, and her emotions. Even though their circumstances appeared to be difficult, they did what was pleasing to God and worked together for a godly outcome, and that's exactly what they were able to achieve.

In 1 Samuel 18–20, we find the story of Jonathan and David, two godly friends working together for the success of the nation of Israel. They understood the importance of working together as spiritual brothers and aligning their minds, choices, and emotions in godly ways so that God's purposes would advance with David as king. Through good times and devastating times, their strong resolve created an environment for God's plan to successfully unfold.

THE COUNTERFEIT

Guarding the soul and dealing with the issue of negative soul ties can be tricky for some people because they may not want to give up certain attachments that are contrary to God's Word. I believe spiritual things have a natural counterfeit. I always say Satan doesn't create, but he can imitate. So, God has created in our soul the wonderful ability for us to have a blessed mind, to use our will to line up with God's will, and to feel His compassion through our emotions. But Satan tries to counterfeit this and twist it into something other than God's highest and best for His people.

In Judges 16, we see a soul connection with a deadly twist. Samson and Delilah attached themselves together in sin and lust. Unfortunately, Samson's purpose for being with Delilah was completely different from Delilah's purpose for being with Samson. One motivation was birthed in love while the other was birthed in hatred. As was the case with Samson and Delilah, soul ties can be strategically disguised. While Samson was a man of God, Delilah was a woman of destruction. From his childhood, Samson had guarded his anointing, his godly strength, and his dedication to God with every fiber of his soul. However, through love, lust, or simply operating in the flesh, Samson let go of the Spirit of God and wisdom—and tied his soul (including his thought life), his physical body, and his spirit to the most ungodly woman in his path.

What happened between Samson and Delilah reminds me of the story of the frog in the pot of water. It is said that if you put a frog into a pot of boiling water, he will immediately recognize the danger and jump out. However, if you put a frog in a pot of cold water and slowly bring the water to a boil, the frog will become comfortable in the slowly warming water and pay no attention to its rising temperature until it's too late. In the same way, Satan works to make sure that things seem comfortable in our lives, keeping us unaware of his tricks and strategies until, before we know it, he starts turning up the heat. But, as long as we are connected to God, the Holy Spirit can change that circumstance by giving us supernatural insight into Satan's hidden agendas.

BE WILLING TO CHANGE

Psalm 139:23–24 says, "*Search me, O God, and know my heart; try me, and know my anxieties; and see if there is any wicked way in me, and lead me in the way everlasting.*" While this sounds so simple and so spiritual, it is not always easy to put into practice. When we are soul-searching to see if God is leading us to change something, many things may come to mind: pride, rebellion, unwillingness to change, and a host of others. How we will respond to them? I often think of the phrase "the path of least resistance." For me, this represents the easy way out. Sometimes, facing the reality of the need to reevaluate a situation also represents the need for change. And for me, personally, change is not the easiest thing to implement. I'm a person of routine, and I like things in order. So any change, even a good one, still represents an adjustment I have to make. Therefore, it would be easy for me to just leave things the way they are. However, if the Lord is leading me to change something, I need to remember He is doing it for my benefit.

SEARCH MY HEART

I did something on purpose in the way I wrote the previous paragraph. I repeatedly used the words *for me*. However, God's highest and best for me could be completely different from what I think is best. And this is where "search my heart" has to be acknowledged. Strong godly women allow God to search their hearts and direct their souls.

Letting God steer the direction of my soul can be the hardest and the easiest thing I have ever done. Obeying God is easy when it's easy. But how about obeying God when it's hard? When our mind, will, and emotions are tied to a particular situation, I believe obeying God in that situation can be difficult, but it is necessary. Yet I believe that, through the power of the Holy Spirit, we can do all things through Christ who gives us strength (Philippians 4:13). The saying "Let go and let God" sounds easy. Sometimes it is, but sometimes it's not. However, letting God teach us how to properly guard our soul and release ourselves from anything unlike Him that is holding us captive may be one of the most important choices we ever make.

> STRONG GODLY WOMEN ALLOW GOD TO SEARCH
> THEIR HEARTS AND DIRECT THEIR SOULS.

SUMMARY

1. I believe we are three-part beings: we are spirit, we have a soul (comprised of the mind, will, and emotions), and we live in a body. When I operate from my soul alone, without having a connection to God in my spirit, my emotions can start to control me and take me in directions I may not want to go. As a believer, I feel the need to feed my soul the nourishing food of the Word of God and let God's Word guide my decisions.

2. Like osmosis, we absorb what we surround ourselves with. I want to be aware of the spiritual infusions I am allowing into my soul—the people and things I am attaching myself to. I encourage you to be aware of

opportunities to connect with godly influences to bring you closer to God in every aspect.

3. In making godly attachments, we can learn a lot about what *not* to do from the outcome of the lives of Samson and Delilah, and we can learn what *to* do by gleaning from the lives of Ruth and Naomi or David and Jonathan. Following godly examples can steer us in the direction of developing godly ties for success.

NOTES TO SELF

Now that you've read this chapter, what notes would you like to write to yourself to help you remember the strength-building points that are most helpful to you or that apply to a specific situation in your life?

_____

_____

_____

_____

_____

WHAT SOME PEOPLE VIEWED
AS JESUS'S FAILURE WAS
ACTUALLY THE GATEWAY TO
FULFILLING HIS PURPOSE—
WITH CONTINUED SUCCESS
THAT CANNOT BE MEASURED.

19

STRONG WOMEN FINISH POWERFULLY

It's not where you start but where you finish that counts.
—Zig Ziglar[1]

This book is about discovering your true strength, your biblical godly strength according to Ephesians 6:10. But I believe that once you discover the godly strength that is in you, it's important to develop it and use it. I pray that as God gives you opportunities to use your strength, you will complete what He calls you to do and finish powerfully. Second Corinthians 8:11 says, *"Now finish the work, so that your eager willingness to do it may be matched by your completion of it, according to your means"* (NIV).

Just before I graduated from college in Florida, I was invited to meet with the college president. He asked me to tell him what I liked most—and what I liked least—about my experience in school. He asked if I was disappointed in what I liked least. I said, "Absolutely not. Sometimes in life, you learn the most from discovering what not to do." While I do appreciate good instruction on what *to* do, to me, learning what *not* to do is also vitally important in any environment.

While I think it has been valuable to give you ideas about what to do to move forward from this point in your life so you can finish strong, a little later in the chapter, I'd also like to give you four things that I find important concerning what *not* to do. I want you to see that no matter where you've been, I believe the most important thing is to finish what you begin, and to finish it powerfully.

Let's look again at Philippians 3:13–15. The apostle Paul penned these profound words:

> *Friends, don't get me wrong: By no means do I count myself an expert in all of this, but I've got my eye on the goal, where God is beckoning us onward—to Jesus. I'm off and running, and I'm not turning back. So let's keep focused on that goal, those of us who want everything God has for us.* (msg)

In 2 Timothy 4:7, Paul wrote, "*I have fought the good fight, I have finished the race, I have kept the faith*" (niv). And he said in Acts 20:24, "*That I may finish my race with joy.*" While I find it so important to finish my race, I also find it important to finish it with joy. I believe that's part of finishing powerfully. In spite of anything you may have experienced in the past that makes you think you're not qualified to move forward, I encourage you that you can move forward and finish your race with joy.

It's important to consider who Paul was when we read these impactful words he wrote. When he was a young man, he was called Saul of Tarsus, and he persecuted Christians (Acts 8:1–3; 9:1–2, 11). He was the one who guarded the coats of those who stoned to death God's beloved messenger Stephen (Acts 7:58).

After Saul went from persecuting Christians to having an experience with the Lord Jesus (Acts 9:3–19), he started to be called Paul and was referred to as an apostle (Acts 13:9; 14:14).

Paul wound up running for his life, hiding from the very people he formerly helped as they persecuted the church. Once God transformed him, he spent the rest of his life preaching the gospel of Jesus Christ and writing much of the New Testament. The lesson here is simple: It's not where you start that matters; it's where you finish. Sometimes getting to the finish line isn't pretty, but the finish line is still the finish line.

So, to help you move past any obstacles that would make you think you aren't capable or even qualified to finish the race, I want to encourage you with four "don'ts" designed to help keep you moving forward. I want you to see that *with* Christ and *through* Christ, you are qualified to do all that He has called you to do. Remember, Philippians 4:13 says, *"I can do all things through Christ who strengthens me"*—not *some* things, but *all* things through Christ who strengthens me.

> WHILE I FIND IT SO IMPORTANT TO FINISH MY RACE, I ALSO FIND IT IMPORTANT TO FINISH IT WITH JOY. I BELIEVE THAT'S PART OF FINISHING POWERFULLY.

HOW TO KEEP MOVING FORWARD

1. DON'T LET YOUR PAST DEFINE YOU

How many of us have wished we could have a do-over? I can't imagine how many times I've wanted a second chance to move forward. Visualize me sitting in a car with a manual transmission. My dad was a car dealer, and I always loved learning about cars. One thing I learned was how to drive a stick shift. I had to manually shift from first gear to second gear to third gear, and so on. I even had to shift into reverse. The car would not shift itself. I had to do it.

Now I'd like you to imagine yourself shifting your mind from the past to the future. Take yourself out of reverse, or even neutral, and see yourself going into first gear, second, third, and finally going forward in every area of your life. I believe the future is right in front of you, just waiting for you to shift from the past into the present and visualize yourself where God has called and created you to be. Focus on your future by looking at Philippians 3:14 and think about pressing forward toward the prize of your high calling, which is in Christ Jesus.

2. DON'T LET SIN DEFINE YOU

First John 1:9 says, "*If we confess our sins, He is faithful and just to forgive us our sins and to cleanse us from all unrighteousness.*" Psalm 103:12 says, "*He has removed our sins as far from us as the east is from the west*" (NLT).

Once you repent and ask the Lord to forgive you for something, why bring it up to Him again? If He has already forgotten it and removed it, it's as though He says to you, "It's already gone. I don't know what you're talking about."

Sometimes people like to remind us of our sins. Maybe you even rehearse your sins to yourself over and over. To obsess over your sin is like refusing to receive all Jesus did for you when He went to the cross. Jesus took nails in His hands and stripes on His back for our healing (Isaiah 53:5). When He went to the cross and was crucified, it was for our total healing and salvation. He paid the price for it all.

In the New Testament, the Greek word *sozo* means "to save." Throughout the Bible, this word is used to mean both salvation and healing—the totality of saving, the saving of all the things you have need of. Jesus took our sins in His own body on the cross, "*(for it is written, 'Cursed is everyone who hangs on a tree'), that the blessing of Abraham might come upon the Gentiles in Christ Jesus, that we might receive the promise of the Spirit through faith"* (Galatians 3:13–14).

Because of what Jesus did on the cross, we can release the sins of the past and walk in the blessing of all that God has for us in the present and the future. This may involve shifting into a new mindset in which we refuse to be defined by our sin, and we choose to move forward.

> ONCE YOU REPENT AND ASK THE LORD TO FORGIVE YOU FOR SOMETHING, WHY BRING IT UP TO HIM AGAIN? IF HE HAS ALREADY FORGOTTEN IT AND REMOVED IT, IT'S AS THOUGH HE SAYS TO YOU, "IT'S ALREADY GONE. I DON'T KNOW WHAT YOU'RE TALKING ABOUT."

3. DON'T LET AGE DEFINE YOU

Considering that I have been around a long time, I have a particular love for not allowing age to define me. So often, young people want to be older, and older people want to be younger. When my daughters were very young, one of them asked my mother-in-law, Evelyn, how old she was. Her answer was priceless: "I'm just right."

I often say that your calling doesn't reflect how old you are but how obedient you are. In Jeremiah 1, the prophet complained to God that he was too young. God paid no attention to his objections. Moses began his public ministry when he was eighty years old. I don't believe God has an expiration date on our calling. He may have a specific timetable for certain things, but I believe what He is primarily looking for is obedience.

4. DON'T LET FAILURE DEFINE YOU

This final step reflects everything I want to emphasize in this book. It's the step to help you understand that, through Christ's work on the cross, you have a right to move forward in your life no matter what you have experienced. Sometimes people try to keep us from moving past our failures. When Jesus hung on the cross, based on the obvious circumstances, people could have viewed His crucifixion as the failure of His mission. But, remember, it wasn't long before Jesus rose from the dead. He fully completed what the Father had called Him to do. And after two thousand years, the continuation of Christianity today is proof that what some people viewed as Jesus's failure was actually the gateway to fulfilling His purpose—with continued success that cannot be measured. If we allow our failures to define us, we can miss what the resurrection power of God can do to give us hope and a future.

SHIFTING GEARS

Think back to me driving that stick-shift car, and again get a visual of what that looks like. Now, begin to see yourself as the driver of your future so you can shift into all that God has for you. I pray that you will have hopeful excitement and anticipation as you see God's plan for you so you, too, can experience Jeremiah 29:11: *"For I know the plans I have for you,' declares the* LORD, *'plans to prosper you and not to harm you, plans to give you hope and a future'"* (NIV).

Because of what Jesus did on the cross, referenced in point four above, here are four action steps that I pray you will embrace to see yourself moving forward into all God has for you. Through Christ, you can be:

1. Strong

2. Fearless

3. Confident

4. Optimistic

Now, as you move forward, I pray that you are strong in the Lord and in the power of His might. Cheer yourself on throughout the journey and believe that God is for you every step of the way.

NOTES TO SELF

Now that you've read this chapter, what notes would you like to write to yourself to help you remember the strength-building points that are most helpful to you or that apply to a specific situation in your life?

CONCLUSION

I have loved writing this book and even found myself growing stronger in my own life through reading many of the pages. I sincerely hope you've come to realize that you, too, can be strong in the Lord and in the power of His might. Let these three key Scriptures be a constant encouragement and reminder of where your *true* godly strength comes from:

> *Be strong in the Lord and in the power of His might.*
> (Ephesians 6:10)

> *I can do all things through Christ who strengthens me.*
> (Philippians 4:13)

> *The joy of the LORD is your strength.* (Nehemiah 8:10)

If you have never asked Jesus into your heart as Savior, or you need to turn back to Him, I encourage you to pray this prayer:

> *Heavenly Father, I come to You right now, and I pray that today is the beginning of a new life filled with Your strength. I*

ask for forgiveness for anything I have ever done that is unlike You. I take Jesus as my Savior and as my Lord. I ask for a brand-new start, strong in the Lord and in the power of His might. In Jesus's name, I pray. Amen.

SPIRITUAL STRENGTH TRAINING: QUESTIONS AND ACTION STEPS FOR EACH CHAPTER

In my observation of dedicated athletes, I find they are diligent to maximize their physical abilities. We can apply the same type of diligence to strengthening ourselves spiritually. So in this section of the book, I invite you to do some strength training for your spirit and soul. As you progress through these questions and action steps, I want to remind you that, throughout this book, I refer to *true* strength as biblical strength based on three particular Scriptures: (1) *"Be strong in the Lord and in the power of His might"* (Ephesians 6:10), (2) *"I can do all things through Christ who strengthens me"* (Philippians 4:13), and (3) *"The joy of the LORD is your strength"* (Nehemiah 8:10). As you think through each chapter and review the questions that pertain to it, I encourage you to approach these questions with faith, believing that God has made you strong and that you can discover and live from your true, godly strength.

Chapter 1: The Power in Choosing Strength

1. What do you believe God has called you to do, and why might you need greater strength from Him in order to do it?

2. Can you list the strength-stealers in your life and how they have affected you?

3. What does it mean to you to choose to "be strong and very courageous" when it comes to what God has called you to do? In what ways do you need to "take courage"?

4. Is the idea of learning to choose your thoughts new to you? What is one situation in your life about which you may need to think differently right now? How can you change your thoughts so you can begin to move toward godly strength?

Chapter 2: Strong Women Understand Their Identity and Their Purpose

1. What aspects about the way God has created you are unique? How do these qualities or abilities affirm that you are "*fearfully and wonderfully made*" (Psalm 139:14)?

2. Have you ever tried to base your identity on what the world says about you when you know it's not what God says about you? How can you continue to build yourself up in God's Word?

3. What is the difference between identity and purpose? How are identity, purpose, and calling connected?

4. Please reread the section "You Are Valuable." What does it tell you about how the world assigns value to people? Why is it essential that we base our value on what God thinks of us?

5. Can you put a specific value on things that God has uniquely done in your life? What aspects of your walk with Christ can you take time to celebrate?

Chapter 3: Strong Women Choose the Word over the World

1. What does it mean to *"seek first the kingdom of God"* (Matthew 6:33)? Have you been waiting for *"all these things"* (verse 33) to be added to you before doing the *"seek first"*?

2. In what way is the substance of your faith like a title deed? What does your faith give you ownership of?

3. What choices do you have when you hear the voices of the world that don't align with God's Word? How can choosing the Word over the world give you strength and position you for receiving God's blessings?

4. As you look through the treasure box of your life, what do you treasure the most? Is there something that gives you exceptional joy? How could you incorporate more of it into your daily life? Is there anything you can share with others to bring them joy?

5. If you had the opportunity to fill a second box from the things in the first box, what are the most important items you would take, and what might you leave behind? Would you add anything to make it more complete, even if it is only a dream?

Chapter 4: Strong Women Go to the Ball

1. Who are the people in your life who give you strength? How do these strength-givers help you stay on God's path?

2. As a believer, why is it so important to be careful of the company you keep?

3. Have you ever taken a chance by going to an event that changed you in a good way—a concert, a church

service, a job interview—ending with a great life-defining moment? Describe this experience.

4. Is there a go-to-the-ball dream or idea in your heart, something you know God wants you to do, but you have hesitated to move toward it for one reason or another? Is that dream worth revisiting? Would you commit that idea to prayer to see where God leads?

Chapter 5: Strong Women Maximize Their Mental Real Estate

1. Is there something you've dreamed of—such as learning to bake, starting a business, taking a class, or doing something to improve your life? Which of your ideas may not just be good ideas but God ideas?

2. What strengths do you have that could help you achieve the ideas God has given you?

3. Have you genuinely and consistently combined your prayers and your faith to believe God for your dreams to become a reality? What are some ways you can do this more effectively?

4. How can you better align your thought life with the truth of God's Word?

Chapter 6: Strong Women Believe in Miracles

1. Reread the story of Oral Roberts. How was his healing actually a group effort?

2. In what area or areas of your life are you believing God to move miraculously?

3. Acts 10:38 says that God anointed Jesus to go around doing good. What are some good things you could do as God anoints you?

4. Oral Roberts coined the phrases "Expect a miracle" and "Something good is going to happen to you." What phrases do you use to encourage yourself to believe God for something good?

5. Do you see yourself as "waiting for the other shoe to drop," expecting something bad to happen—or are you truly expecting a miracle in your life? How can you adjust your thoughts to start believing what Ephesians 3:20 teaches—that God is capable of doing "*exceedingly abundantly*" far above anything we dare ask or think?

Chapter 7: Strong Women Use Their Words Wisely

1. Communication is such a powerhouse. Have you ever thought about the power of the words you're speaking, whether they are good or bad, and how you will have to give an account of them to Jesus? If you truly believe words are powerful, is there anything you need to change about the words you speak?

2. Do you regard the Bible as containing preexisting promises that God is faithful to perform? What areas in your life do you need to turn over to God so you can watch and see how powerful He is according to His Word?

3. Make a list of words and/or phrases that you would like to speak over yourself for encouragement and hope. Make another list of words to speak over other people to bless and encourage them. Try to incorporate this practice into your daily routine.

4. If you had to wear your words, what would you look like? If you had to eat your words, what would they taste like? And if you had to fulfill and walk out your words all day long, what would your day be like? If your words

were to go up like a fragrance in the nostrils of God, what would they smell like?

5. According to the "lemon theory," what words would come out of your mouth if you were in a situation where you were metaphorically squeezed? Why is it so important to hide God's Word in your heart?

Chapter 8: Strong Women Say Yes, No, or Nothing at All

1. What choices in your life are you grateful you made? What choices are you grateful you said no to? Which choices do you wish you could go back to and change your answer?

2. Describe a time when you remained silent and later realized it was the best decision you could have made. Why was it wise?

3. If you are facing some important decisions, consider making a list of those things and handing them over to God, trusting His Spirit to guide you concerning whether you need to say yes, no, or nothing at all.

Chapter 9: Strong Women Listen

1. Please reread Proverbs 4:20. Do you see the importance of listening to life-giving words from good instructors? Who are the wise people in your life you could be listening to?

2. Please reread what Queen Elizabeth said about Jesus Christ. What value can you find in her words that might apply to your own situation?

3. What is "active listening"? Based on what you learned about it, how well do you practice it? How might you need to improve your active-listening skills?

4. What are some ways you can apply what you learned about active listening in your life, not only when it comes to other people but also in listening to God?

Chapter 10: Strong Women Use Their Strengths to Succeed

1. What are three of your greatest strengths?

2. From the strength words listed in this chapter, identify six that best describe your strengths.

3. Which fruits of the Spirit found in Galatians 5:22–23 best describe you? Which ones do you still hope to grow in?

4. How can you make a conscious effort to help build up the strengths of the people around you?

5. Which of the "Seven Rs of Success" are you practicing now, and which do you want to do more work on?

Chapter 11: Strong Women Pursue a Clear Vision for Their Lives

1. Habakkuk 2:2 says, *"Write the vision; make it plain"* (ESV). Has God given you a vision that has not yet come to pass? Consider writing it down and continue to pray.

2. Do you spend a certain amount of time daily in prayer? Even if it's not the same amount of time every day, do you have a plan to be consistent in your time with the Lord?

3. Are there some things in your life you can declutter to allow you to do more productive things for God? Spend time in prayer and ask God what those things might be.

4. What are some ways that you can you practice gratitude and spend time rejoicing in God?

5. How can you personalize the ten steps found in this chapter and make them beneficial to your God-given vision?

Chapter 12: Strong Women Forgive

1. How is Jesus our model for forgiveness?

2. Remember to give the Lord thanks for His continued mercies and kindness.

3. I encourage you to remind yourself of Philippians 4:13: *"I can do all things **through** Christ who strengthens me."*

Chapter 13: Strong Women Know When to Move On

1. Can you remember a time when a strategic exit was one of the most important decisions you ever made? If so, why was it important?

2. Can you remember a time when staying in a certain situation was the right choice, even if it wasn't easy? If so, why was that a great decision?

3. If you sense that God is leading you to move on from a situation, ask Him to show you strategic ways to make your exit peaceful.

Chapter 14: Strong Women Bounce Back

1. The quote from Tim Storey that begins this chapter says, "When you are feeling the sting of a setback, God is preparing you for your comeback." How can a setback turn into a comeback when God is in it?

2. Please reread Isaiah 43:18–19. How do these verses encourage you?

3. Be encouraged as you start your journey taking one step at a time moving forward. It's okay to cheer for yourself and know that God is cheering for you too.

4. How can you actively pray and seek God concerning any "new thing" He has for your life?

Chapter 15: Strong Women Pray

1. When is the best time of day for you to pray? Have you set a specific time to commit to prayer each day? I encourage you to do so, even if you start with just a few minutes.

2. If you mainly pray random prayers, how could you incorporate more specifics into your communication with God?

3. If you were given a task at work, and you had to organize it, would you make a list of what needed to be done? If so, what would be on it? Can you apply the strategy of making lists to your prayers?

4. What is the boomerang prayer? Is there anyone who comes to mind that you could pray a boomerang prayer for?

Chapter 16: Strong Women Give

1. Describe a godly woman you view as strong. In what ways is she generous?

2. In what ways have you been blessed? How can you use these blessings to bless others?

3. What does "paying it forward" mean to you? Can you think of one thing you can pay forward?

4. What does the acronym CHILD stand for? Why is it important to understand that you are part of God's family?

Chapter 17: Strong Women Choose Faith over Fear

1. According to this chapter, what is the relationship between faith and fear?

2. What are four steps you can use to overcome fear?

3. Please take time to read Hebrews 11. What or who in this chapter stands out to you most? Why?

4. What qualities of someone who demonstrates great faith in God can you identify and incorporate into your daily routine?

Chapter 18: Strong Women Guard Their Soul

1. According to Psalm 103:1–5, when we bless the Lord with our soul, what are the benefits that follow?

2. Can you think of times when you have effectively guarded your soul against the wrong kind of influences? How can you further build upon those learning experiences?

3. Please reread David's prayer in Psalm 139:23–24. Make it your own personalized prayer by asking God to search your heart, then work with Him if He is leading you to change something.

4. What practical steps can you take to let God steer the direction of your soul?

Chapter 19: Strong Women Finish Powerfully

1. In this chapter, what caught your attention or seemed important about finishing powerfully? What, in

particular, encouraged you to finish something important to you?

2. List specific Scriptures you can stand on to encourage you to complete a task and finish the job God has called you to do.

3. If you have felt any guilt over not finishing what God has called you to do, consider releasing that guilt right now by accepting God's grace and mercy.

4. I want you to congratulate yourself because, if you've gotten this far, you have almost finished this book! It's my prayer that you are well on your way to becoming *strong in the Lord and in the power of His might* (Ephesians 6:10). Yay for you!

APPENDIX: STRONG WOMAN, IT'S TIME TO THRIVE

*Beloved, I pray that you may prosper in all things and be in
health, just as your soul prospers.*
—3 John 2

Third John 2 is one of my favorite Scripture verses. The apostle John prays for the faithful disciple Gaius to prosper, and I believe that God wants all of us who are faithful to Him to prosper as well. It's important to realize that prosperity is not an end in itself; it's meant to be the result of a quality of life, a commitment, a dedication, and actions that are in line with the Word of God. We can see that this is true in Gaius's case as we read further in 3 John. He is commended for walking in truth (verse 3) and love (verse 5) and for showing generosity and hospitality (verses 5–6).

The English word *prosper* comes from the Greek word *euodoo*, which means "to help on the road"; "to succeed in reaching"; "to succeed in business affairs"; "to have a prosperous journey."[1] According to *MerriamWebster.com Dictionary*, to prosper means "to become strong and flourishing" or "to cause to succeed or thrive."[2] And the Online Etymology Dictionary says that to prosper means "to be successful, thrive, advance in any good thing."[3] These definitions clearly imply that true biblical prosperity is not a momentary, passing phenomenon but rather an ongoing state of success.

I believe God intends for every believer's soul (mind, will, and emotions) to experience true biblical prosperity in every area of their lives, so they can be whole and complete in Him, *"lacking nothing"* (James 1:4).

"Just as" is an interesting phrase in 3 John 2. It appears between two phrases that are directly proportional to each other. John prays that as Gaius's soul prospers, he would equally prosper in all other areas of his life. Perhaps this is why we are to guard our mind, will, and emotions so carefully.

We can see that Gaius's faithfulness in service to God, along with his generosity, prompted John's prayer for him to prosper not only spiritually but in other ways as well. This is in line with 2 Corinthians 9:8: *"And God is able to bless you abundantly, so that in all things at all times, having all that you need, you will abound in every good work"* (NIV).

If I were given an opportunity to preach a message from a portion of the Word of God that I viewed as an all-encompassing Scripture, I would seriously consider using the message of 3 John 2 because I believe it helps us to see what a lavish, giving Father our God is.

The true message of biblical prosperity is about discovering and becoming acquainted with God's ways of doing and being, then emulating His ways. This puts us into position to receive all that God has for us as we walk out His plan for our lives. And we can rest assured that God's plans for us are good and for our benefit and not for harm (Jeremiah 29:11).

The Bible has much more to say on the subject of prosperity than just 3 John 2. The words *increase, prosperity,* and *prosper* occur in the King James Version more than 100 times. In the Old

Testament, *"prosper"* is translated from the Hebrew word *tsalach,* which means "to break out," "to come mightily," "to go over," "to be good," "to be meet," "to be profitable," "to cause to prosper," "to effect prosperity."[4]

I pray this book has helped you discover your true, godly strength, and my desire is that you continue to grow in godly strength daily. I feel so passionate about your prospering and succeeding in every area of your life that I want to conclude this book with some Bible verses about all the good things the Lord desires for you as His child. I hope you'll consider memorizing and even basing your everyday prayers for yourself and others on them because I believe they are so *powerful.*

JOSHUA 1:8

This book of the law shall not depart out of thy mouth; but thou shalt meditate therein day and night, that thou mayest observe to do according to all that is written therein: for then thou shalt make thy way prosperous, and then thou shalt have good success.   KJV

Study this Book of Instruction continually. Meditate on it day and night so you will be sure to obey everything written in it. Only then will you prosper and succeed in all you do.   NLT

2 TIMOTHY 3:16–17

All Scripture is given by inspiration of God, and is profitable for doctrine, for reproof, for correction, for instruction in righteousness, that the man of God may be complete, thoroughly equipped for every good work.   NKJV

All Scripture is inspired by God and is useful to teach us what is true and to make us realize what is wrong in our lives. It corrects us when we are wrong and teaches us to do what is

right. God uses it to prepare and equip his people to do every good work.   NLT

PROVERBS 4:20–22

My son, attend to my words; incline thine ear unto my sayings. Let them not depart from thine eyes; keep them in the midst of thine heart. For they are life unto those that find them, and health to all their flesh.   KJV

Dear friend, listen well to my words; tune your ears to my voice. Keep my message in plain view at all times. Concentrate! Learn it by heart! Those who discover these words live, really live; body and soul, they're bursting with health.   MSG

JOHN 10:10

The thief cometh not, but for to steal, and to kill, and to destroy: I am come that they might have life, and that they might have it more abundantly.   KJV

The thief comes only to steal and kill and destroy; I have come that they may have life, and have it to the full.   NIV

3 JOHN 2

Beloved, I wish above all things that thou mayest prosper and be in health, even as thy soul prospereth.   KJV

Beloved, I pray that all may go well with you and that you may be in good health, as it goes well with your soul.   ESV

PSALM 68:19

Blessed be the Lord, who daily loadeth us with benefits, even the God of our salvation.   KJV

Praise be to the Lord, to God our Savior, who daily bears our burdens.   NIV

ROMANS 8:32

He that spared not his own Son, but delivered him up for us all, how shall he not with him also freely give us all things?

KJV

If God didn't hesitate to put everything on the line for us, embracing our condition and exposing himself to the worst by sending his own Son, is there anything else he wouldn't gladly and freely do for us?   MSG

JAMES 1:17

Every good gift and every perfect gift is from above, and cometh down from the Father of lights, with whom is no variableness, neither shadow of turning.   KJV

Every good and perfect gift is from above, coming down from the Father of the heavenly lights, who does not change like shifting shadows.   NIV

PSALM 37:3–4

Trust in the LORD, and do good; so shalt thou dwell in the land, and verily thou shalt be fed. Delight thyself also in the LORD: and he shall give thee the desires of thine heart.   KJV

Trust in the LORD and do good. Then you will live safely in the land and prosper. Take delight in the LORD, and he will give you your heart's desires.   NLT

1 CORINTHIANS 14:33

For God is not the author of confusion, but of peace.   KJV

When we worship the right way, God doesn't stir us up into confusion; he brings us into harmony.   MSG

JAMES 1:5

If any of you lack wisdom, let him ask of God, that giveth to all men liberally, and upbraideth not; and it shall be given him.   KJV

If any of you lacks wisdom, you should ask God, who gives generously to all without finding fault, and it will be given to you.   NIV

JOHN 14:1

Let not your heart be troubled: ye believe in God, believe also in me.   KJV

Do not let your hearts be troubled (distressed, agitated). You believe in and adhere to and trust in and rely on God; believe in and adhere to and trust in and rely also on Me.   AMPC

PSALM 29:11

The LORD will give strength unto his people; the LORD will bless his people with peace.   KJV

The LORD gives his people strength. The LORD blesses them with peace.   NLT

PHILIPPIANS 4:13

I can do all things through Christ which strengtheneth me.
    KJV

For I can do everything through Christ, who gives me strength. NLT

PSALM 4:8

I will both lay me down in peace, and sleep: for thou, LORD, only makest me dwell in safety. KJV

In peace I will lie down and sleep, for you alone, O LORD, will keep me safe. NLT

JOHN 14:27

Peace I leave with you, my peace I give unto you: not as the world giveth, give I unto you. Let not your heart be troubled, neither let it be afraid. KJV

Peace I leave with you; my peace I give you. I do not give to you as the world gives. Do not let your hearts be troubled and do not be afraid. NIV

1 PETER 5:7

Casting all your care upon him; for he careth for you. KJV

Give all your worries and cares to God, for he cares about you. NLT

2 THESSALONIANS 3:3

But the Lord is faithful, who shall stablish you, and keep you from evil. KJV

But the Lord is faithful; he will strengthen you and guard you from the evil one. NLT

PSALM 37:23

The steps of a good man are ordered by the L<small>ORD</small>, *and He delights in his way.*   <small>NKJV</small>

The L<small>ORD</small> *makes firm the steps of the one who delights in him.*   <small>NIV</small>

PROVERBS 12:2

A good man obtains favor from the L<small>ORD</small>.   <small>NKJV</small>

Good people obtain favor from the L<small>ORD</small>.   <small>NIV</small>

JEREMIAH 17:14

Heal me, O L<small>ORD</small>, *and I shall be healed; save me, and I shall be saved, for You are my praise.*   <small>NKJV</small>

Heal me, L<small>ORD</small>, *and I will be healed; save me and I will be saved, for you are the one I praise.*   <small>NIV</small>

PSALM 103:2–5

Bless the L<small>ORD</small>, *O my soul, and forget not all his benefits: who forgiveth all thine iniquities; who healeth all thy diseases; who redeemeth thy life from destruction; who crowneth thee with lovingkindness and tender mercies; who satisfieth thy mouth with good things; so that thy youth is renewed like the eagle's.*

<small>KJV</small>

Praise the L<small>ORD</small>, *my soul, and forget not all his benefits—who forgives all your sins and heals all your diseases, who redeems your life from the pit and crowns you with love and compassion, who satisfies your desires with good things so that your youth is renewed like the eagle's.*   <small>NIV</small>

PHILIPPIANS 4:19

But my God shall supply all your need according to his riches in glory by Christ Jesus.   KJV

And this same God who takes care of me will supply all your needs from his glorious riches, which have been given to us in Christ Jesus.   NLT

2 CORINTHIANS 9:8

And God is able to make all grace abound toward you; that ye, always having all sufficiency in all things, may abound to every good work.   KJV

And God is able to bless you abundantly, so that in all things at all times, having all that you need, you will abound in every good work.   NIV

PSALM 23:1

The LORD is my shepherd; I shall not want.   KJV

The LORD is my shepherd, I lack nothing.   NIV

PSALM 34:10

The young lions do lack, and suffer hunger: but they that seek the LORD shall not want any good thing.   KJV

The lions may grow weak and hungry, but those who seek the LORD lack no good thing.   NIV

PSALM 147:3

He healeth the broken in heart, and bindeth up their wounds.   KJV

He heals the brokenhearted and binds up their wounds. NIV

2 CORINTHIANS 5:17

Therefore if any man be in Christ, he is a new creature: old things are passed away; behold, all things are become new.
KJV

Therefore, if anyone is in Christ, the new creation has come: The old has gone, the new is here! NIV

JOHN 16:24

Hitherto have ye asked nothing in my name: ask, and ye shall receive, that your joy may be full. KJV

Until now you have not asked for anything in my name. Ask and you will receive, and your joy will be complete. NIV

NOTES

Chapter 1: The Power in Choosing Strength

1. "Do Not Strive in Your Own Strength—Andrew Murray," Deeper Christian Quotes, May 4, 2020, https://deeperchristianquotes.com/do-not-strive-in-your-own-strength-andrew-murray/.

Chapter 2: Strong Women Understand Their Identity and Their Purpose

1. Eleanor Miller, "How Ancestry.com Makes Money," *Business Insider*, January 30, 2012, https://www.businessinsider.com/how-ancestrycom-makes-money-2012-1.

Chapter 3: Strong Women Choose the Word over the World

1. Aakash Khatter, "Existentialism," Medium, August 20, 2018, https://medium.com/@aakashkhatter1296/existentialism-630e80610671#:~:text=Existentialism%20is%20a%20philosophical%20theory,through%20acts%20of%20the%20will.

2. *Merriam-Webster.com Thesaurus*, s.v. "hell," accessed March 15, 2024, https://www.merriam-webster.com/thesaurus/hell.

Chapter 4: Strong Women Go to the Ball

1. Max Lucado, *In the Eye of the Storm* (Nashville, TN: Thomas Nelson, 1991), 84.

Chapter 5: Strong Women Maximize Their Mental Real Estate

1. Billy Graham, *Wisdom for Each Day* (Nashville, TN: Thomas Nelson, 2019), 201.

2. Mary Bellis, "Charles Darrow and the Monopoly of Monopoly," ThoughtCo., May 30, 2019, https://www.thoughtco.com/monopoly-monopoly-charles-darrow-4079786.

Chapter 6: Strong Women Believe in Miracles

1. *The Oxford Pocket Dictionary of Current English*, s.v. "destruction," Oxford University Press, in Encyclopedia.com, May 18, 2018, https://www.encyclopedia. com/literature-and-arts/language-linguistics-and-literary-terms/english-vocabulary-d/destruction.

Chapter 7: Strong Women Use Their Words Wisely

1. "Pilot Speak Aviation Codes Refresher," Small Airport FBO Free Newsletter, February 2021, https://www.businessaircraftcenter.com/articles/pilot-aviation-language-code-art0221.htm.

Chapter 8: Strong Women Say Yes, No, or Nothing at All

1. "Decimius Magnus Ausonius" Quotes, A-Z Quotes, https://www.azquotes. com/author/28906-Decimius_Magnus_Ausonius.

Chapter 9: Strong Women Listen

1. Mind Tools Content Team, "Active Listening: Hear What People Are Really Saying," Mind Tools, n.d., https://www.mindtools.com/az4wxv7/active-listening.

2. Queen Elizabeth II, "Christmas Broadcast 2016," British Royal Family website, December 25, 2016, https://www.royal.uk/christmas-broadcast-2016.

3. Camilla Tominey, "World Exclusive: Sophie, Countess of Wessex—Why the Queen Inspires Me," *Express*, October 18, 2015, https://www.express.co.uk/ news/royal/612253/World-Exclusive-Sophie-Countess-of-Wessex-The-Queen-interview.

4. Lindsay Roberts, *Discover Your True Worth* (Nashville, TN: Emanate Books, 2022), 125.

5. Mother Teresa, *In the Heart of the World: Thoughts, Stories, & Prayers*, ed. Becky Benenate (Novato California: New World Library, 1997), 19.

Chapter 10: Strong Women Use Their Strengths to Succeed

1. *The Oxford Pocket Dictionary of Current English*, s.v. "strength," Oxford University Press, in Encyclopedia.com, May 18, 2018, https://www.encyclopedia. com/strength.

2. *The Oxford Pocket Dictionary of Current English*, s.v. "resolve," Oxford University Press, in Encyclopedia.com, https://www.encyclopedia.com/humanities/ dictionaries-thesauruses-pictures-and-press-releases/resolve.

3. *The Oxford Pocket Dictionary of Current English*, s.v. "receive," Oxford University Press, May 23, 2018, in Encyclopedia.com, https://www.encyclopedia.com/ receive.

Chapter 11: Strong Women Pursue a Clear Vision for Their Lives

1. Terri Savelle Foy, *Imagine Big: Unlock the Secret to Living Out Your Dreams* (Ventura, CA: Regal Books, 2013), 11.

2. Merriam-Webster.com Dictionary, s.v. "clutter," accessed February 17, 2024, https://www.merriam-webster.com/dictionary/clutter.

Chapter 12: Strong Women Forgive

1. Corrie ten Boom, "Guideposts Classics: Corrie ten Boom on Forgiveness," *Guideposts*, November 1972, https://guideposts.org/positive-living/guideposts-classics-corrie-ten-boom-forgiveness/.

Chapter 13: Strong Women Know When to Move On

1. Evan Woodbery, "Justin Verlander Bids Farewell: I Had '45 Minutes to Make Hardest Decision of My Life,'" MLive, September 1, 2017, https://www.mlive.com/tigers/2017/09/justin_verlander_video_message.html.

Chapter 14: Strong Women Bounce Back

1. Tim Storey, "4 Ways to Survive Your Darkest Days," Oprah.com, n.d., https://www.oprah.com/inspiration/how-to-cope-with-tragedy.

2. Oscar Hammerstein II, "Do-Re-Mi," 1959.

Chapter 15: Strong Women Pray

1. E. M. Bounds, *Purpose in Prayer* (New Kensington, PA: Whitaker House, 2019), 103.

2. See *Strong's Exhaustive Concordance of the Bible*, G1573.

Chapter 16: Strong Women Give

1. Jennifer Leigh Selig, ed., *What Now? Words of Wisdom for Life After Graduation* (Kansas City, MO: Andrews McMeel Publishing, 1999), 171.

2. *Strong's*, H974.

Chapter 17: Strong Women Choose Faith over Fear

1. Elisabeth Elliot Foundation, "Faith does not eliminate questions. But faith knows where to take them," Facebook, February 1, 2021, https://www.facebook.com/elisabethelliotfoundation/photos/a.116322013432459/240669324331060/?type=3.

2. Oxford Languages, s.v. "faith," from Google's English dictionary, "define faith" keywords search, Google.com.

Chapter 18: Strong Women Guard Their Soul

1. *The Oxford Pocket Dictionary of Current English*, s.v. "infusion," Oxford University Press, in Encyclopedia.com, https://www.encyclopedia.com/medicine/divisions-diagnostics-and-procedures/medicine/infusion.

Chapter 19: Strong Women Finish Powerfully

1. Zig Ziglar, A Z Quotes, https://www.azquotes.com/quote/808663.

Appendix: Strong Woman, It's Time to Thrive

1. *Strong's*, G2137.

2. Merriam-Webster.com Dictionary, s.v. "prosper," https://www.merriam-webster.com/dictionary/prosper.

3. *Online Etymology Dictionary*, s.v. "prosper," https://www.etymonline.com/search?q=prosper.

4. *Strong's*, H6743.

ABOUT THE AUTHOR

Lindsay Roberts is a minister, writer, editor, sought-after speaker, wife, mother, and lifelong student of the Bible. She is the host of the inspirational women's television program *Make Your Day Count* and the *Entirely Unconventional* podcast. Lindsay also cohosts, with her husband, Richard, *The Place for Miracles*, a half-hour interactive broadcast that reaches millions of households worldwide. She is editor and publisher for Oral Roberts Ministries publications, which includes her *Make Your Day Count* online magazine, and she is the author of numerous books, including *Discover Your True Worth*. Lindsay and Richard have three daughters and live in Tulsa, Oklahoma.